GHOST TOWNS AND FORGOTTEN PLACES OF NORTHWEST ARKANSAS

GHOST TOWNS AND FORGOTTEN PLACES OF NORTHWEST ARKANSAS

HEATHER WOODWARD

Foreword by J.P. Wellington

Published by The History Press
An imprint of Arcadia Publishing
Charleston, SC
www.historypress.com

First published 2025

Manufactured in the United States

ISBN 9781467170154

Library of Congress Control Number: 2025940393

This book is dedicated to all of those who came before me whose stories made it in this book. May your memories live on. I see you, I hear you. You are not forgotten.

CONTENTS

Foreword, by J.P. Wellington 9
Acknowledgements 13
Introduction 15
A Brief History of Northwest Arkansas 19

PART I: GHASTLY GHOST TOWNS
Rush 31
War Eagle 42
Peppersauce 55

PART II: LOST LANDMARKS
Monte Ne 61
Dinosaur World 72
Dogpatch USA 76
Arkansas Tuberculosis Sanatorium 84

PART III: FORGOTTEN FACES
Crescent Hotel 95
Trail of Tears Park 127

Conclusion 133
Bibliography 137
About the Author 141

FOREWORD

Some places disappear quietly. Others leave echoes.

The ghost towns and forgotten places scattered across Northwest Arkansas don't always look like ruins. Sometimes, they're submerged beneath lakes, sometimes reduced to nothing more than a field with a name. Sometimes, they're half-intact buildings with boarded windows and no story on record. But every one of them has a heartbeat if you know how to listen.

I've spent over two decades studying the folklore, cultural remnants and backwoods histories of the Ozarks, and I can tell you this: the land remembers. Long after the last resident is gone and the final train departs, something lingers. A feeling. A pull. A fragment of who we were, buried under time but not entirely lost. These places are not just abandoned; they are paused, waiting to be remembered.

That's what Heather Woodward has done here. She has remembered them.

In *Ghost Towns and Forgotten Places of Northwest Arkansas*, Heather offers more than a travel guide. She offers a resurrection. She steps into hollowed-out towns and their half-submerged dreams to give them voice again. She doesn't romanticize or sanitize what's left. There's no attempt here to tidy up history or ignore its rough edges. She brings grit and grace in equal measure, telling the truth as it is, with the kind of reverence that doesn't require perfection.

Heather's approach is unique. She's not just a researcher. She's a storyteller, a seeker and someone who walks into the forgotten and asks questions most people don't bother with anymore. She explores places like Monte Ne—not just its submerged amphitheater but also the wild ambition behind it.

She looks at War Eagle Mill—not just its remaining structure but also the layers of overlooked history it represents. And she doesn't stop at well-known sites. She digs deeper, uncovering places like the Booneville Tuberculosis Sanatorium, where thousands lived, died and were quietly erased from public memory.

This is not passive reading. Heather brings you with her. You're standing beside her on muddy paths and overgrown trails. You're peeking through boarded windows. You're looking at old photographs that no longer have names written on the back. She makes you feel the loss. The wonder. The weight.

What makes this book stand out is its balance between fact and feeling. Yes, you'll get the history, the dates, the buildings, the names. But you'll also get the mood, the energy, the things left unsaid in the records. This is history written with a pulse. It's for people who believe that cemeteries have character, that buildings can hold memory and that folklore isn't just myth, it's the emotional record of a place.

There's a growing hunger these days for stories that don't make it into the mainstream. More and more, we want to understand the weird and the overlooked. The histories that weren't celebrated, the towns that didn't survive, the people whose lives didn't end up in textbooks. This book answers that hunger. It fills in some of the blanks. It doesn't give all the answers, but it gives something better: a reason to look closer.

Heather's writing reminds me of the old storytellers I grew up with in the hills. Folks who could recall not just who lived in a house but also what kind of pies they baked or which nights the porch light was always left on. There's a detail-oriented intimacy here that doesn't come from reading historical markers; it comes from spending time with the places themselves. Listening. Wandering. Letting the story unfold rather than forcing it.

If I had to describe this book in one word, I'd say it's *haunting*. Not in the scary movie sense—though there are ghost stories here, too—but in the way it stays with you. You'll be thinking about these towns days after you put the book down. You'll start wondering what happened to that half-collapsed barn you passed on Highway 23. You'll begin to see silences in the landscape differently.

And that's the point, I think.

This book is a call to remember, not just in a historical sense but in a spiritual one. To remember what was here before the parking lots and the subdivisions. To remember the communities that lived and died without fanfare. To remember that Arkansas is more than what you see on the welcome sign. It's the layers underneath.

There's a kind of sacred work in remembering the forgotten. It's not glamorous. It doesn't come with medals or applause. But it matters. Because the land we walk on holds more stories than we can possibly know, and each one we uncover brings us closer to understanding who we are and where we came from.

Heather Woodward has done that work. And in sharing it with us, she invites us to join her. To slow down. To look closer. To pay attention to the rusted signs, the foundations peeking out from lakes, the names etched into concrete before the water came.

So, take a deep breath before you turn the page. What you're about to read is part historical record, part ghost story, part love letter to a place that has given so much and asked for so little in return.

But more than anything, it's a reminder: just because something is forgotten doesn't mean it's gone.

J.P. Wellington
Writer, Researcher
April 2025

ACKNOWLEDGEMENTS

Thank you to all of the curious people in my life who jumped in the car with me and went on adventures without asking a lot of questions: Mom, Sarah, Stephanie, Chris and the now-defunct Op Slither.

INTRODUCTION

A PLACE TIME FORGOT (BUT I DIDN'T)

Northwest Arkansas has always had strange energy. It's something passive unless you're really paying attention. It's not loud like the cities, and it's not still like the flatlands. It hums in the hollows. It whispers through the trees. It vibrates through old stone foundations. If you've ever stood in the middle of nowhere, halfway down a gravel road with no GPS signal, and you've gotten a gut feeling that something used to be there, you know exactly what I mean.

This book is for that feeling.

It started with curiosity. I didn't set out to write a book. I just wanted to know what happened to certain places I'd heard about in passing, read about in articles or learned about through ghost tours. What I found wasn't just history. It was strange little echoes of the past that refused to be completely erased.

Some of these places are buried beneath lakes. Others are overgrown, crumbling or slowly being reclaimed by the woods. A few are still standing, propped up by stubborn locals or the occasional preservation effort. But they all have stories.

Ghost towns capture something primal about the human spirit. They're physical evidence of lives once lived, people who built homes, raised children, ran businesses, laughed, fought, loved and left. Sometimes, their reasons for leaving are clear: floods, fires, the collapse of the mining industry. Other times, it's less obvious. Maybe a railroad skipped them. Maybe the soil gave out. Maybe people just stopped showing up.

An Enslaved Cemetery in Fayetteville. *Photo by author.*

But even when the people are gone, the energy lingers. You can feel it in the way the air shifts when you step inside a rotting building. You can see it in the crooked headstones no longer visited. You can hear it, sometimes, in the creak of an abandoned staircase or the rustle of leaves that seem to move without wind.

In Northwest Arkansas, ghost towns aren't always complete shells. Sometimes, they're partially inhabited. A building here, a road there, maybe one old resident that's been around long enough to remember when it was all thriving. You'll find these remnants tucked into the folds of the Ozarks, hanging on by rusted nails and rotting foundations.

Alongside the classic ghost towns, I've included what I call "lost landmarks," spots that aren't totally abandoned but are often overlooked or misunderstood. Monte Ne is a perfect example. It wasn't a failure in its time, but its ambition outpaced reality. Now, it's mostly underwater, with just enough ruins poking out to spark questions.

The Booneville Sanatorium is another. It's not on every ghost hunter's list, and yet it carries layers of medical history, loss and local legend. These places may not be on postcards, but they've shaped the land and the people who came after.

And then there are the quirky corners of our cultural past, like Dogpatch USA and Dinosaur World. While they're technically not ghost towns, they've got the bones of dreams that didn't quite pan out. They tell a different kind of story: not of survival or tragedy but of kitsch, capitalism and the strange charm of failed amusement.

The wheel at the War Eagle Mill.
Photo by author.

WHAT YOU'LL FIND IN THIS BOOK

This isn't a comprehensive list of every ghost town in the region. It's a curated selection based on places I could visit, the research I could find (which is sometimes harder to find than I expected) or the firsthand accounts I could get. Some chapters are heavy on history. Others lean into the weird. Many sit right at that intersection where historical fact and local folklore blur into each other.

Each chapter pulls you into the spirit of a place: what it was, what it became and what it left behind. I've included photos where I could, interviews when available and local stories that don't always line up with official records (the locals always have better tales).

While this book is rooted in research—yes, I've gone through archives, interviewed locals, read historical accounts—it's also deeply personal. I've walked through these places. I've felt their silences. I've gotten lost more times than I can count trying to find a road in the middle of nowhere. And I've stood in more than one empty structure thinking someone's still there, wanting someone to tell their story.

I love facts. But I also believe that feelings, folklore and firsthand stories deserve a seat at the table, especially when we're dealing with places that have been forgotten—not because they weren't important but because they were inconvenient to remember.

WHO THIS BOOK IS FOR

If you've ever slowed down to look at an abandoned building and wondered what happened there, this book is for you.

If you grew up in Northwest Arkansas and want to reconnect with pieces of its past that aren't in the tourist brochures, this book is for you.

If you're drawn to eerie things, to stories with loose ends, to places that seem to vibe with something just beneath the surface, you're in the right place.

And if you're just here for the history? Great. There's plenty of that, too. I promise I didn't make anything up (though I can't promise that the locals didn't).

And one last note. This is the way I heard it. Or read it. Or experienced it. If you've lived in the area all your life and you heard it a different way, that's amazing. But that doesn't mean I'm wrong. It just means we had different experiences. I'll honor yours if you honor mine.

A FINAL NOTE BEFORE WE BEGIN

Northwest Arkansas is changing fast. Towns are expanding, rural spaces are filling up and once-forgotten places are being rediscovered, rebranded or erased. Some of the sites in this book may look different by the time you read this. (Monte Ne comes to mind.) You can visit a lot of these places, but a lot of them are permanently closed, their history forgotten.

That's partly why I wrote this book. To preserve what's left. To document what I could. To give these places one last moment to speak. Because even in silence, they matter.

A BRIEF HISTORY OF NORTHWEST ARKANSAS

Before Northwest Arkansas was home to Walmart executives, this land was part of a vast wilderness that supported Native tribes who lived off the forests, rivers and limestone bluffs.

The Osage were the dominant force in the region, though other tribes, like the Caddo, Quapaw and Tunica, moved through the area. The Osage Nation had a reputation: they were proud, fiercely territorial and skilled at both hunting and diplomacy. Their territory stretched from Missouri into Kansas, Oklahoma and Northwest Arkansas. They didn't build permanent towns here, but they returned seasonally to hunt deer and bear, trap beaver and gather plants along the White River basin. The Osage referred to themselves as *Ni-u-kon-ska*, or "Children of the Middle Waters," a nod to their connection with the rivers that ran through their homelands.

In the 1600s and 1700s, European colonizers began traveling through the Ozarks, trading metal tools, guns and alcohol for animal pelts. First, it was the French. Then it was the Spanish. And then the French came again. Everyone seemed to think they had a claim to this land, whether the people who actually lived here agreed.

By the early 1800s, the Osage were in constant negotiations with the U.S. government over treaties they didn't write and land they didn't want to sell. The Louisiana Purchase, in 1803, officially made Arkansas part of the United States, at least on paper. In reality, it was still Osage country. That didn't stop settlers from flooding in, armed with land grants and a pioneer spirit, all backed by the full weight of manifest destiny.

In 1808, the Osage were pressured into signing the Treaty of Fort Clark, ceding most of Missouri and northern Arkansas. Then came the Treaty of 1818, which shoved them even farther west. They were relocated to what is now Kansas and later Oklahoma, forced to abandon the land their ancestors had walked on for generations.

And just like that, Northwest Arkansas became a place for settlers. They built roads to make traveling more accessible. They planted homesteads and fenced off what had once been open land. What had been sacred hunting grounds and river crossings became the sites of general stores, churches and dusty town squares. The Osage were gone—but not by choice. And the new residents, for the most part, didn't care or look back.

The irony is, even today, much of Northwest Arkansas still bears the imprint of the Osage, whether people realize it or don't. Place-names like Osage Creek, Osage Mills and even Osage Drive on Google Maps are all left in plain sight. The rest is buried in the soil or tucked away in museum archives.

It's easy to start a story with white settlers and Civil War skirmishes, but the truth is, this land had a full-blown history long before Arkansas had a state flag. The Osage and the tribes who came before them treated the land as sacred, not something to be owned, flipped or subdivided.

By the time statehood rolled around in 1836, most of the Native presence in Northwest Arkansas had been erased or relocated. The Trail of Tears, one of the darkest chapters in American history, would soon pass through this region, bringing other tribes like the Cherokee, Creek and Choctaw on their forced march westward.

Fayetteville, now the cultural hub of the region, started as a basic military outpost. In 1828, a land office opened to handle all the eager settlers pouring into Washington County, staking claims on property that had, just years earlier, belonged to the Osage and other tribes.

Fayetteville was officially founded in 1835, just one year before Arkansas became a state. The original town square was built up with brick buildings, saloons, a few mercantile shops and a whole lot of mud. Churches popped up as fast as blacksmith shops, and by the time Arkansas joined the Union in 1836, Fayetteville was already a central point in the region.

Thirty miles north, Bentonville had a quieter start. It was originally known as Osage, named after the tribe who had once hunted there. In 1837, a new post office opened, and the town was renamed for Missouri Senator Thomas Hart Benton, a fan of westward expansion. Bentonville officially became the county seat of Benton County in 1836 and would go on to become a hub for agriculture, legal disputes and, eventually, Walmart.

THE CIVIL WAR IN THE OZARKS

By the time the Civil War rolled into Arkansas, the state was already dealing with problems: limited infrastructure, scattered towns and a tense relationship with the federal government. But when the Confederacy formed in 1861, Arkansas signed up early. The decision split the state right down the middle, and this was most obvious in Northwest Arkansas.

If you're imagining uniforms, battlefields and orderly troop movements, this wasn't that kind of war. In the Ozarks, the Civil War played out more like a family feud with muskets. Brothers fought brothers. Uncles fought against nephews. Most families were divided.

In March 1862, the Union army clashed with Confederate forces just northeast of Bentonville in what would become one of the most significant battles west of the Mississippi, The Battle of Pea Ridge.

Roughly twenty-six thousand troops fought across hills, forests and frozen ground. Union General Samuel Curtis held off the Confederate army, led by Earl Van Dorn, despite being outnumbered. Union forces controlled the high ground and supply lines. After two days of fighting, the Confederates retreated, and the Union secured northern Arkansas for good.

It was a decisive victory, one that helped keep Missouri in Union hands and pushed the Confederacy farther south. But for the locals, it meant farmland turned into battlefields, barns used as field hospitals and homes burned down as punishment or strategy.

The scars didn't go away. You can still visit Pea Ridge National Military Park today. The battlefield looks eerily preserved, but don't be mistaken, blood was spilled there, and it shaped the political future of the region.

Pea Ridge might've been a big headline, but the real terror came from something less organized: guerrilla warfare.

Bushwhackers (pro-Confederate fighters) and Jayhawkers (pro-Union fighters) roamed the hills, ambushing wagons, stealing livestock and burning down homes. There were no uniforms, no rules of engagement, just neighbors turning on neighbors with rifles and torches.

In towns like Fayetteville, Springdale and Cane Hill, entire families were displaced. Churches and schools were shut down. Some towns were burned to the ground and never rebuilt. The war didn't just divide communities; it gutted them.

Even after the Union "secured" Northwest Arkansas, raids continued. In April 1863, the Confederate forces actually launched a surprise attack on

Fayetteville, attempting to reclaim it. They were repelled, but the message was clear: no place was truly safe.

Most Arkansans didn't enslave people. The few who did typically lived in the southern and eastern parts of the state. But that didn't stop men from enlisting on both sides. Some joined out of loyalty to their state, others joined due to family pressure and plenty joined because the army offered food, clothing and a paycheck.

The conscription laws didn't help. Both Confederate and Union forces forced young men to fight. Those who resisted were often jailed or worse. In many Ozark households, one brother joined the Union, the other the Confederacy. It wasn't just a civil war, it was a personal war.

When the war finally ended in 1865, Northwest Arkansas was a mess. The infrastructure was gone. Homes were in ruins. Towns like Fayetteville and Bentonville had to be rebuilt from almost nothing.

Many families never returned. Entire communities disappeared. Some towns, like Maysville and Richland, never bounced back. Others, like Fayetteville, were slowly rebuilt, thanks to education, railroads and new commerce.

The war changed how people saw each other. Old alliances broke. Distrust lingered. And for decades after, Northwest Arkansas was known as a place with a long memory and short temper when it came to politics.

The people of the Ozarks didn't just survive the Civil War; they came out of it with a chip on their shoulders and a fierce sense of independence. You can still feel it in the landscape. In the way small towns guard their traditions. In the stories passed down like heirlooms. The war ended. The rebuilding began. But the wounds ran deep.

AFTER THE CIVIL WAR

After the Civil War, Northwest Arkansas was battered, broken and burned. Like a stubborn weed pushing through cracked pavement, the region began to rebuild. Slowly. Awkwardly. And with a lot of help from iron rails and steam engines. In the 1870s and 1880s, nothing changed a town's fortune faster than the railroad. It wasn't a mayor or a preacher who could put a place on the map. It was a train.

The St. Louis–San Francisco Railway, better known as the Frisco Line, was the catalyst for real change in the Ozarks. By 1881, the Frisco was laying tracks deep into Northwest Arkansas, linking little mountain towns with big cities like St. Louis, Memphis and, eventually, Dallas. For a rural, recovering region, this was a lifeline. Trains meant goods could come in and, more importantly, go out. Farmers could sell apples and sorghum syrup in Chicago. Timber mills could ship lumber to Kansas City. Even tiny towns like Winslow and West Fork suddenly had a reason to exist.

Fayetteville, still licking its wounds from the war, jumped at the chance to rebuild. The University of Arkansas opened its doors in 1871, helping anchor the city as an educational hub. But it was the railroad that made it viable.

The Frisco arrived, and Fayetteville got a depot and a direct line to the outside world. Hotels sprang up near the tracks. New businesses opened. Lumber, livestock and produce could finally reach real markets. Some towns were born because of the railroad. Springdale, for instance, exploded in the late nineteenth century, thanks to its location on the line. It became a major shipping point for apples and other produce.

Rogers was another railroad baby. It didn't even exist until 1881, when the Frisco decided it needed a depot between Lowell and Avoca. Once the trains started stopping there, the town sprouted almost overnight. By 1900, it had general stores, a newspaper and a population in the thousands.

On the flipside, towns the railroad skipped, like Elm Springs and Brightwater, faded into the background. Some became ghost towns. Others just stalled. In the railroad age, proximity to the tracks meant life or death. It wasn't just about commerce. Trains brought people. New settlers arrived looking for cheap land, fresh starts, or business opportunities. Immigrants from Germany, Italy and eastern Europe started putting down roots in Northwest Arkansas, often bringing skilled trades or new farming techniques with them.

The railroad also brought in tourism. People from St. Louis or Little Rock could hop a train to the Ozarks for a "health retreat" in Eureka Springs or Monte Ne. Suddenly, the woods weren't just for locals; they were a destination. And for better or worse, railroads also brought modernization. Telegraph lines followed the tracks. Mail delivery improved. The concept of "on time" took on new meaning. For a region that had been operating on church bells and seasonal rhythms, the trains brought clocks, contracts and capitalism.

While the Civil War was fought with rifles, in the postwar era, economic wars were fought with rail lines. Competing towns tried everything to get on a route, offering land, tax breaks and outright bribes to railroad companies. Local leaders would practically grovel to get a depot. That scramble shaped the layout of Northwest Arkansas. Towns that won the railroad lottery are still here. Towns that lost are now little more than names on a map or have been forgotten altogether.

AGRICULTURE, APPLES AND THE RISE OF THE TYSON EMPIRE

Before Walmart put Bentonville on the map, before Razorbacks flooded Fayetteville on game day, Northwest Arkansas was all about farming—and not just any farming. The area's main crop was apples. For decades, the region was covered in orchards. Apple trees stretched across the hills like a patchwork quilt, and Springdale was the heart of it all.

The shift from fruit to fowl wouldn't happen overnight, but when it did, it changed everything. As apples were dying, chickens were multiplying. By the 1940s, the focus had shifted to poultry. The climate, terrain and access to rail shipping made Northwest Arkansas ideal for chicken farming. And nobody took that potential more seriously than John W. Tyson.

Tyson moved to Springdale in the 1930s and started hauling chickens to Kansas City. He saw a gap in the market and filled it quickly. What began as a small feed-and-haul operation turned into Tyson Foods, officially incorporated in 1947. While the rest of the country was dealing with postwar supply issues, Tyson was perfecting vertical integration. That means the company controlled everything from hatcheries to feed mills to processing plants. If you were in Springdale in the 1950s, chances are good that someone in your family worked for Tyson.

By the 1970s, Tyson was a national player. By the 1990s, it was a global giant. Today, it's one of the largest meat producers in the world. Poultry wasn't the only game in town. Washington and Benton Counties also produced beef, soybeans and dairy. But chickens ruled the roost, and poultry contracts reshaped the local economy. Farmers became growers under Tyson contracts, raising birds to corporate specs and timelines.

The model was efficient but not without controversy. Labor conditions, environmental concerns and economic dependency became hot button issues. Still, Tyson brought jobs, infrastructure and a level of national relevance the region hadn't seen since the apple days. Other companies followed suit. George's Inc., Simmons Foods and Ozark Mountain Poultry all set up shop, turning the Ozarks into a protein powerhouse.

Through all the changes, one thing stayed constant: the land. People still farmed. Families still passed down land like a sacred heirloom. Even as agriculture industrialized, the identity of Northwest Arkansas remained rooted in the soil. You can still find old orchards tucked behind strip malls. You'll still see coops and tractors parked next to $600,000 townhomes. And you'll still meet folks who can tell you exactly when the last apple packing house in their county shut down.

THE UNIVERSITY OF ARKANSAS AND CULTURAL SHIFTS

If the railroad gave Northwest Arkansas its momentum, the University of Arkansas gave it its mind. Tucked into the hills of Fayetteville, the university didn't just bring books and professors. It brought ideas, art, protest, innovation and a steady flow of outsiders who didn't look, think or vote like everyone else. In a region known for its small-town roots and rural identity, this was revolutionary.

The University of Arkansas was born in 1871, just six years after the Civil War ended. The state legislature was under pressure to provide a public university, and after a bidding war between towns, Fayetteville won out. The deciding factor came when the town offered land, money and a view. The university was built on a hill overlooking the town, later known as "The Hill."

The first classes were held in a single building called Old Main, a brick behemoth that still stands today. At the time, there were eight students and three professors. But from day one, the goal was clear: educate Arkansas's future leaders and elevate the region beyond farming and frontier life.

The university grew and so did its presence. By the early 1900s, sports were a big deal, especially football. In 1910, the school changed its mascot from the Cardinals to the Razorbacks after coach Hugo Bezdek said his team "played like a wild band of razorback hogs." The symbol stuck and gave the university a unique identity. You don't have to look far in Fayetteville to see razorback statues, bumper stickers or pig-themed puns.

But it wasn't just about football. The university became a cultural anchor. With the university came libraries, theaters, art galleries and a flood of academics. It gave Fayetteville a liberal, intellectual core in the middle of a largely conservative, rural state.

In the 1960s and '70s, the campus became a hotspot for political activism. Students protested the Vietnam War, fought for civil rights and pushed for women's equality. The free speech movement reached The Hill, and the idea that Fayetteville could be more than just a college town started to take hold.

The university also houses an MFA creative writing program, considered one of the best in the country, producing literary talent that's reshaped modern fiction. Thanks to the university, Fayetteville slowly morphed from a backwoods college town into a culturally rich, progressive hub. It's home to music venues, art walks, experimental theater, indie bookstores and more food trucks than you can count.

And while it still has its roots in Southern tradition—football tailgates, church on Sunday and a love for biscuits—it also has drag shows, poetry slams and environmental activists. The contrast isn't just tolerated. It's kind of the whole point. Fayetteville is the kind of place where you might overhear a conversation about climate change, crypto and SEC rankings all in the same coffee shop.

The university didn't change just Fayetteville; it lifted the entire region. Students brought families. Families brought businesses. Businesses brought opportunity. And suddenly, you had an economy that wasn't just based on chickens, cows and commodity prices. Even towns that aren't technically college towns, like Springdale or Rogers, benefited from the jobs, research and workforce that flowed out of the university.

Today, the University of Arkansas is one of the biggest employers in the state. It enrolls over thirty thousand students and continues to shape the political, cultural and economic future of Northwest Arkansas.

HOW WALMART TOOK OVER THE OZARKS

If you'd told someone in 1950 that tiny Bentonville, Arkansas, would one day become a global business epicenter, you probably would've been laughed out of the feed store. But then came Sam Walton, and everything changed.

Walmart didn't just reshape Bentonville. It rewired Northwest Arkansas's economy, identity and skyline. The town that once depended on apples and dry goods is now home to corporate headquarters, executive jets, world-class museums and a staggering number of Teslas per capita.

In 1950, Sam Walton bought a modest variety store on the Bentonville town square. He called it Walton's 5 & 10, and it was nothing fancy. But Sam had a knack for business and a nose for what rural folks actually wanted: low prices, decent selection and convenience.

By 1962, he opened the first Walmart Discount City in Rogers. It was a gamble. Discount retailing was still a new concept, and Northwest Arkansas was hardly a bustling metro. But Sam's bet paid off. People drove from counties away to shop. The prices were unbeatable, the stores were sprawling, and the empire began to grow. Walmart's growth was fast, aggressive and relentless. By the 1980s, the company had expanded across the South. By the 1990s, it was going national. And by the 2000s, it had gone global.

Walmart's headquarters stayed rooted in Bentonville. It was part tradition, part strategy. The company's frugality and rural origin story were part of its branding. But as Walmart became one of the largest corporations on Earth, the sleepy town had to grow fast. Soon, Bentonville wasn't just a town, but it was also a command center. Thousands of employees worked in the company's maze of office buildings. Executives flew in from around the world. Suppliers moved in just to stay close to the mothership.

If you wanted your product in Walmart stores, you needed boots on the ground in Bentonville. That's why you'll find satellite offices for companies like Procter & Gamble, PepsiCo, Nestlé and countless others right here in the Ozarks. The population exploded. So did the housing prices. And suddenly, Bentonville wasn't just on the map; it was a global address.

The shift wasn't subtle. Mom-and-pop diners made way for upscale bistros. Locals who used to drive tractors now dodged Range Rovers in traffic. Art installations popped up where auto shops used to be. Coffee got fancier. Jeans got tighter. Rent got a lot more expensive.

The heirs of Sam Walton, especially Alice Walton, have poured money into transforming Bentonville into something most locals never imagined: a cultural destination. Alice founded Crystal Bridges Museum of American Art, a massive, high-tech, world-class museum tucked into the woods just outside of downtown. Admission is free, thanks to Walmart money.

Then came The Momentary, a contemporary art space in a repurposed Kraft cheese factory. Then there were bike trails, sculpture gardens, gourmet restaurants, luxury hotels and Whole Foods. Love it or hate it, Walmart is the economic engine of Northwest Arkansas. It supports tens of thousands of jobs, directly and indirectly. It's a reason the region has lower unemployment and higher growth than most rural areas. But it also brings baggage. There are labor controversies, wage debates, environmental questions and an ever-widening wealth gap. Bentonville now has both million-dollar estates and trailer parks within a ten-minute radius. Still, Walmart turned the region into something few saw coming: a place with power, influence and global reach. Northwest Arkansas transformed from the backwoods to billionaire row in less than a century.

PART I

GHASTLY GHOST TOWNS

RUSH

The Buffalo River National River Park
Yellville, Arkansas

Note: The Rush Historical Center is sixteen miles south of Yellville.

Rush is the only ghost town situated between the Mississippi River and the Rocky Mountains. It's located in the Buffalo River National River Park, just outside of Yellville, Arkansas.

In the 1880s, prospectors came to the area looking for the lost silver mines talked about in Native lore. They found an abundance of metallic flakes concentrated in the rocks, which they wrongly assumed was silver. Word of mouth traveled fast, and soon, a small town was built up in the mountains to facilitate the many men who thought they would strike it rich.

In 1886, a rock smelter was constructed to start the extraction process of the metallic substance. In January the following year, during a test run of the smelter, green zinc oxide fumes dashed the hopes and dreams of all of those who thought there was silver in the Arkansas hills.

Even though many prospectors did not want the claim of the area anymore, a man named George Chase bought it and created the Morning Star Mine. By the 1890s, the company became known as the biggest and most popular mining operation in all of Arkansas. Throughout the years, seventeen other mines inhabited the area, including the Lucky Dutchman, Dixie Girl, Monte Cristo and Red Cloud. Zinc mining dominated the area.

The Rush, Arkansas sign. *Photo by Sarah Woodward.*

Prospectors and laborers migrated to the area to create their fortunes. However, toiling in the mine came with a cost. Working conditions were grueling and hazardous, and the days were long. Accidents and cave-ins were frequent. Many workers contracted respiratory diseases, like typhoid pneumonia. Miners had to haul ore by wagon over rough roads to Summit or Buffalo City, where it was shipped to Joplin, Missouri, for smelting.

Makeshift tent cities popped up in the hills of rural areas and garnered the name "rag towns." Sewage seemed to always be an issue in these rag towns, and the fear of getting typhoid ran rampant. The area needed growth in order to press on. To accommodate the newly thriving industry, businessmen traveled to the area to build infrastructure for its burgeoning populations. This included hotels, barbershops, a community pool, a supply store and a post office. By 1916, there were over five thousand people living in the area, and documents were filed to incorporate an official city, Rush.

During the 1892 Chicago World Fair, the Morning Star Mine received blue ribbons for its nugget of zinc oxide that weighed thirteen thousand pounds. The mine won more blue ribbons at the 1904 St. Louis World Fair for another large nugget of zinc oxide.

At the end of World War I, zinc oxide prices declined rapidly, and the town of Rush dwindled. By World War II, the Morning Star Mine had shut down its operations, and the processing mills were dismantled for salvage. Many of the inhabitants of Rush moved away to find work elsewhere.

The post office closed its doors sometime in the 1950s, which officially ended the town's identity. In 1972, Rush was officially declared a ghost town and was included as part of the Buffalo National River Park system.

One of the more prominent structures in Rush was the Hicks property, a ten-acre plot that housed the family, a livery, a hotel and a general store. In 1915, the two-story store and inn held prominence in the area because it was the only building made of stone, a sign of wealth at the time. The Hicks family persevered and remained in the town longer than most during its recession. Their store continued operations until the early 1940s, and the hotel burned down in the 1950s. Eventually, the store building was renovated into a family residence and remained that way until the end of the town. Today, only the fieldstone retaining wall, the staircase and some remnants of the store remain. The Hicks plot has been digitally reconstructed by the Historic American Landscape Survey (HALS) and the ESRI Story Map, giving visitors a glimpse of what it looked like in its heyday.

The Rush ghost town was listed in the National Register of Historic Places on February 27, 1987. Unlike the structures in most ghost towns, the original buildings and structures of the failed city are fully intact and taken care by the park system. There are trails that you can hike that will take you to some of the more remote areas of the town, including some of the mines. However, you cannot tour the mines due to safety issues.

GOING TO RUSH, ARKANSAS

Rush is out in the middle of nowhere. I don't say that lightly. I live in a small town with a population of about two thousand. I have been told that I live in the middle of nowhere, but Rush does not compare. There's a Walmart and a McDonald's in my town. I have high-speed fiber internet and a great cellphone reception. I am hardly living in a desolate area. Rush, on the other hand, is the true nowhere.

According to online directions, the ghost town is located sixteen miles outside of Yellville, which has a population of about one thousand. It's a "blink and you will miss it" town that holds very little amenities beyond a local grocery store and a Dollar General. Once you leave the area, the land becomes more rural, with houses strewn between farmland and trees.

The old dilapidated general store. *Photo by Sarah Woodward.*

To get to Rush, you have to turn down a windy road that goes deep into the forest. You are literally out in the middle of nowhere. If you are going to visit, make sure to bring snacks, water and anything else that is a must-have. There is no cellphone reception in the area—not even a single bar. It's a dead zone.

Also, be aware that the roads are not well paved. There are areas that are packed with dirt and gravel. If possible, drive a car with four-wheel drive or a vehicle with good tires. You are basically one step away from off-roading.

Rush is situated in the middle of a National Forest. To get to the mines, to see the sinkholes and to tour the ruins of the town, you have to hike through a lot of rugged trails. So, wear comfortable clothing and good walking shoes.

As you get closer to the ghost town, you will see an official sign that says "Rush" on it. Then after about a mile, there are two sets of old dilapidated houses. These are the homes that are all over the internet. The first set of buildings are three wood residential houses behind a makeshift wire fence. The second set are the rickety remnants of the general store and the post office. They are also located behind a wobbly wire fence.

Booths were moved to a flat area for viewing. They are the only full buildings that are left in the town, aside from the blacksmith barn that you can view during the self-guided hike through the original layout of the mining town.

As you drive about a quarter of a mile, you will see the main site of Rush. There is a small parking area with displays about the Rush and the zinc mines. There are steps that go straight up to the ruins of the Morning Star Mill. You can also walk a more leisurely path that will go up the mountain to the ruins. Either way, the path goes around in a circle. So, it doesn't matter which way you go. You will end up seeing all the remnants of the ghost town.

At around the halfway mark of the circular route, you can veer onto another path that goes to the opening of the Morning Star Mine. According to the marker there, the hike is about a tenth of a mile long. However, be forewarned that it goes up a steep incline on a craggy path that feels like it goes nowhere. It's worth the hike once you get to the top, but it will feel like it takes forever.

Once you got up to the top of the path, you will see a ventilation hole. A lot of people think that's the entrance to the mine, but it's not. You have to walk a little bit farther to a fence; inside is the opening. It's boarded up with metal slats because the mine is caved in.

If you keep walking a little farther, there is a second entrance to the mine. It's also boarded up because it's caved in. However, you can get closer here and have a more tactile experience.

After you get through the circular hike through downtown Rush and witness the mills and the mine, you can stop there. Or you can drive another mile and check out the old stone foundation of the McIntosh Mill. The exquisite masonry of the stone walls still stands, and it's quite a sight to see.

If you drive another mile, you will end up at Rush Landing. There, you can swim or kayak in the Buffalo River. Or you can take a two-mile hike through the outskirts of Rush, which housed other mines. There are foundations of some of the mills, sinkholes and more entrances to other mines. The end of the trail dumps off at the Morning Star Mine opening.

EXPERIENCING RUSH

I went to Rush with my mom, my sister and my boyfriend. After we traipsed through the woods, followed the trails, visited the mine openings and took the circular walking tour, I asked our motley crew what they thought of the experience. This is the transcription of our conversation I recorded on a voice recorder.

> ***Heather**: I need your experience at the Rush Ghost Town. Everybody.*
> ***Mom**: There was no energy. It was dead. It was neutral. There was like nothing there going on. It was cool, like, visually and to see what it was, but, like, I was looking for energy, and I didn't feel anything.*

Heather: *If you were going to come here, what would you tell people?*
Chris: *It's a part of history. That, and don't expect too much 'cause there's not a lot to see, but it's cool. It's definitely cool to see. It's something that was and isn't. I just think it's cool to see they put a lot of effort into making this place, and then it just disappeared.*
Mom: *Yeah, it disappeared. It's weird, like, that was insanely expensive in their time. That probably cost millions to make those buildings; they took masons to make those stones.*
Sarah: *It's pretty. I can see why it's lost and forgotten. I could hang out here. There isn't any energy here. It's, like, weird.*
Heather: *It's peaceful?*
Mom: *Yeah, it's peaceful. It's not scary at all. I don't know why. I don't know how there was a whole town here, and then there's no energy.*
Heather: *Do you think it's weird that there's no energy and there was a whole town here?*
Mom: *I do. I think it's very strange, because either the people were very spiritually awakened or the nature cleared it. It's very void of energy of anybody living here. Yeah. Like you don't feel like there was ever a town here. It just feels—I don't know—maybe they were really good people that lived here. I thought the mine would at least have some energy to it. People died in the mine, and maybe their intention was pure. Maybe it was a really nice group of people that lived here and they had pure intentions, and then it just cleared when they left. A lot of towns like Deadwood, when you go to them, it was like there was a lot of evil going on and greed. Maybe that wasn't the case with people here.*
Chris: *Yeah. But there's still, like, big companies coming in—*
Mom: *Yeah. But it's not the same, as maybe they were really legit companies, and they treated their people right. It wasn't like they were trying to exploit and profit off of them. Maybe it wasn't like that kind of a energy. 'Cause it doesn't feel like there was anything here that's very agitated. It just feels like they packed up and left, and they took their energy with them. I wouldn't know if people lived here if I didn't see the ruins. It just feels unadulterated, and the nature took it back over.*
Heather: *You think nature just healed itself?*
Chris: *If you go up to the mine, there's rubble everywhere,* [but] *nature just took over. Plants grew, trees grew, took everything over. Maybe there wasn't anything unresolved.*
Sarah: *Could be—*

What's left of the McIntosh Mill.
Photo by author.

Mom: *That's usually when there's residue of energy left over, because things were left undone or unresolved, or there was unjustness, or they could also have died really quickly and not suffered.* [If] *you have a bunch of rocks falling on you, if you get squished, there's no suffering. And most of those weird spirits that stick around suffered. But even the ground is not like sad. I've gone to other mines. You can feel the energy of the earth, the spirit of the place kind of being marred or broken. Maybe they did it in a very gentle way. Although blasting through a mountain is pretty aggressive. I don't even feel like there's any haunting either. It's not feeling haunted at all. I do feel an Indian thing. More than I do the white people.*

Heather: *But living here was rough. You lived in tents, you didn't have bathrooms, you didn't have any kind of amenities. You walked up a hill to get to the mine. You worked underground. You came out with all kinds of lung problems.*

Chris: *It's not like coal mining.*

Heather: *Yeah. But the pneumonia—*

Mom: *You should look up zinc or whatever they were mining. Maybe there's some healing properties to it. Zinc is really good for you, and maybe the zinc was something that contributed to what was going on here.*

Sarah: *If I had the internet, I would, but we don't have the internet here.*

***Mom**: I'm about sure you'll find something about zinc. It could have contributed to the culture here and how people interacted with each other.*

[When I got home, I did, in fact, find out something about zinc. Here are the metaphysical properties: it's a transformational stone. It can help you deal with sudden changes. It's the stone of geologists and miners. The stone can be used to help banish grief and sorrow.]

***Mom**: Like, for instance, when the witch hunts were going on, they said that a lot of people were being affected by the mold in the wheat. It was causing people to hallucinate. They were getting high from the—I forgot the name of it—but there was something in the wheat that was psychedelic, and they ate it cause it rotted, and then they got high and they thought they were witches. Also, there was a lot of rats and rat feces mixed in with it. Just think about how that affected the whole culture of that area. So, maybe the zinc here affected the area just as much. You never know.*
***Heather**: There were thirteen mines up here at one time, and they all got along. You think so?*
***Mom**: It doesn't feel like there was any kind of feuding or anything. It's just like business. It's "get down to business and do* [what] *we need to do and make everybody happy." It just feels like the energy here was very amicable. But it's weird that they just got up and left, too. You just leave the town. "We're done now."*
***Chris**: 'Cause there's no work. There's no money. People have to go make a living* [and] *be able to support their families. And all the buildings are gone. It was good for a while, and then when it wasn't good anymore, they left. But it seems like the whole town was based around the mine. Maybe I'll give them to America. Maybe there might have been more to it.*

MY EXPERIENCE AT RUSH, ARKANSAS

In my almost thirty years of investigating, I have been to a good amount of ghost towns and unincorporated areas. Most of them were really haunted. The one that has stuck with me and reminds me a lot of Rush is called Brunckow's Cabin—except it's ridiculously haunted.

The cabin is named after Frederick Brunckow, who developed a silver mine about eight miles outside of Tombstone. He built his cabin to accommodate his mining operation. Between 1860 and 1890, twenty-one people were killed in or near the cabin, and most were buried on site. This kill count gave the structure the title "the bloodiest cabin in Arizona's history."

To get to the cabin, you have to trek across the desert for about thirty minutes. Some of it is located on private property. It's not a fun walk. There aren't any roads. It's craggy, desolate and hilly. Right before you get to the cabin, you have travel down a hill into a creek. There's no other way to get to the other side, where the foundation and the walls of the cabin stand.

Every time I've brought investigators to the area, everyone has gotten sick in that wash. People double over in pain and feel nauseous. They always want to go back, forgetting they are about a mile and a half from civilization. It's the weirdest phenomenon.

Once you get past the wash and go up the other side of the hill, you will walk on a trail a while longer. You pass mine openings and the foundation of an alleged mill. There's one mine opening just before the cabin ruin. It's

An air vent in the Morning Star Mine. *Photo by Sarah Woodward.*

allegedly where Brunckow was murdered with his own mining drill. It's an awfully creepy location, and nobody ever wants to stay there long. This is all before you even get to the cabin.

The activity there is even worse. There are shadows that move. Voices. Feelings of being watched. Rocks that come flying at you out of nowhere. The feeling of evil is everywhere, and it makes your stomach drop. It's a nerve-wracking experience. The first time I went to the cabin, I thought it was an anomaly. However, I went back three or four more times with different people, and the activity replicated itself time and time again.

If you are in Tombstone and want to have an eventful experience, the following is the latitude and longitude of the cabin:

Latitude: 31.63857°, or 31° 38' 19" north
Longitude: -110.15753°, or 110° 9' 27" west

Google it, and you will find directions from investigators who have been there. Or you can ask the locals in Tombstone. They will give you good directions. Either way, prepare for an interesting hike.

That's what I thought Rush was going to be like. I thought it would have that ominous feeling of the bruised and broken earth. The eerie tattered energy of the mine accidents and the deaths of miners. The eerie whispers of the lost and forgotten.

But that's not what happened. Nothing happened, actually.

The Buffalo River Creek. *Photo by Sarah Woodward.*

The remnants and ruins of Rush are some of the most peaceful, quiet places I have ever been. They're nestled in the beautiful Ozark backwoods. The Buffalo River is just up the road; the townspeople used it for baptisms.

The sun was out. The sky was blue. The wind rattled through the trees. It was a beautiful spring day. Not a negative vibe was felt.

Even at the mine openings. Shards of rubble and piles of rock were strewn about on the sides of the mountain. There were definitely signs of explosions. The side of the mountain was marred and cracked open.

But sitting on the ground, feeling out the energy of the place, it felt quiet. Resolved. It's such an interesting area. It's beautiful and broken with the shards and remnants of time passed. It's a moment in history that time has seemingly forgotten, nestled in the woods off the beaten path.

WAR EAGLE

11004 War Eagle Road
Rogers, Arkansas 72756

War Eagle is the oldest community in Benton County. It used to be a small burgeoning town of industry and community. Now, it's a small unincorporated area known for the histories of its mills and steel and wood bridge. The name of the community comes from the War Eagle Mill on War Eagle River.

In 1873, the town had its first community hub: a general store. The store was sold in 1882 and extended to become a meeting place and post office. In 1961, the store burned down, and in 1967, the post office closed. Across the way, another general store cropped up in 1900, but it closed its doors in 1959. The store's building still stands. Now, the War Eagle Mill has the only store in the area. It sells flour products and tourist memorabilia.

THE VAN WINKLE MILL

In the 1840s, Peter Van Winkle moved to Northwest Arkansas. He founded a series of successful businesses in Fayetteville and then decided to branch out into the lumber business. He built a steam-powered mill and created an empire with over eight thousand acres of timber.

War Eagle. *Photo by Sarah Woodward.*

In 1862, the Civil War hit Northwest Arkansas. Van Winkle buried $4,000 on his property and moved his family to Texas. After the war, the entrepreneur came back to Arkansas. He found his mill burned down and his gold dug up. He didn't let the setback get him down, and he set his sights on rebuilding. Van Wrinkle rebuilt his home and took the opportunity to create a saw and gristmill with a 150-horsepower steam engine.

Getting the parts of the steam engine to War Eagle was feat in itself. The three boilers were manufactured in St. Louis, Missouri. They were shipped by barge down the Mississippi River and then up the Arkansas River to Van Burn. Then the boilers were carried by oxen through the mountains.

The twenty-four-foot flywheel was cast in sections and then shipped to the nearest railroad stop in Rolla, Missouri. The pieces were brought to Van Winkle on a wagon with twelve mules. The entrepreneur assembled all of the wheel pieces together by himself on his property.

When all the components were put together, the steam engine powered two molding saws, a circular saw, two rip saws, two molding saws, a shingle main, a lathe and two planers. The mill went into production right away, and its products helped Northwest Arkansas recover after the destruction from the wear. It produced lumber, doors, cabinets, windows, molding and balusters.

In 1871, the University of Arkansas established its first permanent structure, Old Main, in Fayetteville. All of the lumber for the structure came from Van Winkle's mill. By 1880, the mill had produced over 1.3 million pieces of lumber.

Van Winkle died in 1882, and his son-in-law, J.A.C. Blackburn, took over the business. Blackburn did so well with the business that he became known as the "lumber king of Northwest Arkansas." By 1889, he had acquired over seventeen thousand acres of land. The mill was closed in 1890. In 1919, the mill was plundered by a group of robbers, who took dynamite to the flywheel and then sold the parts for scraps.

In 1928, Blackburn sold the mill land to Roscoe Hobbs, who founded the Ozark Tie Co. He manufactured thousands of railroad ties. In 1968, Hobbs died, and the land was sold to the State of Arkansas. The Hobbs State Park was created in 1979; it has 12,056 acres of land and still stands.

THE WAR EAGLE MILL

In 1832, Sylvanus Blackburn and his son traveled from Tennessee to Arkansas to scout land that was being sold for five cents an acre. He ended up buying 160 acres, his new homestead, for eighty dollars. During the winter, Blackburn moved his entire family to the parcel, including his wife, Catherine; his children; his parents; some of his extended family; and some enslaved people. The Blackburn family stayed in tents on the land and built a two-story home.

In 1835, the Blackburns built the water-powered War Eagle Mill. The mill had a waterwheel, which powered the grist stones, turning corn, wheat and other grains into flour and meal. To control the water flow of the War Eagle River, the Blackburns built a small dam that is still used today.

The mill provided a community space for news and trade. Settlers would come from miles around to have their grains milled, and while they did this, they would also socialize and pick up supplies. To accommodate the growing community, the Blackburns built a general store and a building that doubled as a school and Masonic lodge.

In 1848, the mill was washed away during a flood. However, the Blackburns rebuilt and kept business going until the Civil War. Blackburn took his family to Texas—like his Van Winkle neighbors—to keep them safe. Their five sons joined the Confederate army.

In 1862, two days before the Battle of Pea Ridge, the Confederate army burned down the War Eagle Mill so it would not be taken over by the Union. The family home was used as a headquarters for a Confederate general and, later, a Union general. Thus, it was spared.

The mill was built for the third time by J.A.C. Blackburn in 1872, this time with a cast-iron water-powered turbine that ground grain and drove

The War Eagle Mill. *Photo by Sarah Woodward.*

a sawmill. During this time, Blackburn ran both mills: the Van Winkle mill and the War Eagle Mill.

In 1890, Catherine Blackburn died. Sylvanus asked his sons to dig a grave large enough for two people. Five days later, he died and was buried in the same plot as his wife.

By 1900, the mill had stopped its production and was left in disrepair. In 1903, A.E. Crossman bought the dilapidated structure and replaced its timber dam with a concrete one that still exists today. Once again, the mill burned down in 1924 and was left in disrepair. During this time, the Blackburns' home was turned into the War Eagle Hotel.

In 1973, Leta and Jewell Medlin and their daughter, Zoe Cawood, bought the mill property and restored it to its old glory. The fourth inception of the War Eagle Mill is a replica of its 1873 iteration. It's the only fully functional gristmill in Arkansas and the only undershot water-powered mill in the United States.

In 2004, Elise and Marty Roenigk bought the property, and the mill still grinds grain like it did before the Civil War. You can visit the War Eagle Mill at 11045 War Eagle Road, Rogers, Arkansas, 72756.

THE WAR EAGLE BRIDGE

In the 1900s, the War Eagle River, when the water was high, could be crossed only by ferry; when the water level was low, people could cross the river on foot. The community around the mill burgeoned, and a more robust, streamlined transportation system was needed to cross the water. In 1907, a 182-foot-long, 40-foot-wide steel bridge was commissioned for the price of $4,709 to accommodate the new growth. The bridge was listed in the National Register of Historic Places in 1985.

THE WAR EAGLE CAVERN

Situated four miles from the mill, the War Eagle Cavern has three levels and unusual features, like domes, waterfalls and rimstone dams. The cave spans just short of two miles and has an underground canyon that stands one hundred feet tall. It is the oldest cave in Arkansas and the largest in Northwest Arkansas.

The cavern was officially opened to the public in 1978. However, the Native population in the area used it long before for housing. During the Civil War, soldiers used the cavern to retreat to during battles to get some much-needed respite. Moonshiners used the waters in the cave to make hootch during Prohibition.

Before the crash of the stock market in 1929, which caused the Great Depression, Arkansas encountered a disastrous flood. In 1930, the state was hit by a devastating drought. During this time, the cave system was used by families who had lost their homes. It was an attractive shelter mainly due to its consistent flow of fresh water.

In 2023, the War Eagle Cavern property went through some renovations. General manager Guy Schiavone worked with his team to open more cave passageways. He said that the work had to be done by hand, shoveling debris into wheelbarrows and buckets. All the backbreaking work created about two hundred more feet of cavern for the tour.

Over the years, many people who used the cave as a dwelling etched their names into the walls. During the excavation of the new parts of the cavern, Schiavone found a name that tied 150 years of the area's history together.

Here's what Schiavone had to say:

Top: War Eagle Bridge. *Photo by Sarah Woodward.*

Bottom: The War Eagle Cavern Gift Shop. *Photo by Sarah Woodward.*

> *So we were down there one day. We're figuring out where are we going to install the light fixtures and where are we going to put this walkway. As we were doing that, we looked over at the wall and said, "Hey, there's some scratches on the wall right there." Then I looked closer at it, and I said, "That says 'Blackburn.' Isn't that the guy who built the War Eagle Mill down the road?"*

The Blackburn family built the mill and kept the community together for the pivotal years of War Eagle. This means that at some point, the Blackburn family had gone through those caves. "This entire region, all of us here in this part of Northwest Arkansas, we're all linked and we're all connected to each other," said Schiavone.

GOING TO WAR EAGLE

War Eagle is another tiny community out in the middle of nowhere. It's nestled in a corridor of backroads just outside of Hobbs State Park. Without the bright red, three-story mill, anyone could drive right by it and not realize that anything interesting ever happened there. It's literally a "blink and you miss it" community.

Across from the parking lot of the War Eagle Mill is a dilapidated, wooden shack with a rickety porch that is something straight out of a horror movie. Of course, I had to go look at it. When I drove up to it, I realized there was a broken-down street that turned a corner and went somewhere off in the distance. Went I drove up it, on both sides of the road were older houses. They looked like they had been there for years. There were more roads and more houses. A quiet little neighborhood that had weathered the years and still quietly thrived. An older couple with sincere smiles in their eyes as they waved at me.

Even though the neighborhood stands in plain sight, it's not noticeable. I think this is because nobody expects there to be people living on these backroads that are mostly framed by lush fields of grass and farmland, where there are more cows than humans. However, this area was a little haven for commerce at one point. But you wouldn't know it now, with the meager number of cars that drive over the bridge. One car every five to ten minutes. Mostly travelers from Rogers cutting through the area to get Highway 412. And then a smattering of tourists looking for the bridge and the mill because they probably saw a picturesque postcard from the area.

I live only thirty minutes from War Eagle Mill, yet I previously had no idea of its history. I have driven by the mill a handful of times on my way to Rogers or to a more desolate part of Beaver Lake. In my mind, it was just part of scenery. Something cute and kitschy that went with the landscape. The same goes for War Eagle Cavern, which is four miles away. I have driven by it so many times and never thought to pull into the driveway to look around.

There are so many little pocket communities in this area that hold so much rich history and ingenuity. The Blackburns and the Van Wilders were

The War Eagle Mill machine. *Photo by author.*

just normal people with dreams and a vision. They took their hard-earned money and risked everything to hopefully create some kind of legacy. Luckily, there were others around who recognized the importance of their story and what they created. They are now immortalized in the mill gift shop.

When you walk into the War Eagle Mill, the first floor of the wooden building holds the gift shop and the grinding area. There are bags of different kinds of flour, pancake mixes, bread mixes, flavored syrups, candy and cooking amenities. At the opposite end of the room, there is a section for the grinding mechanisms that are attached to the giant wheel at the side of the building.

There are signs that explain the entire process, and there is a mirror that shows you what is inside the grinder chute. Usually, the wheel is turning and the grain is being milled in real time. However, I went one morning after a large stormfront had gone through Northwest Arkansas. The skies were still overcast and threatened with more rain. The War Eagle River swelled and snaked rapidly through the terrain. The salesperson at the counter said that the water was too high and too choppy for the wheel to work properly, so they had to keep it off. It was still fascinating to look at all of the independent pieces and then see how they worked together in tandem through the diagrams and visual aids plastered everywhere.

Near the counter, there were pictures of the Blackburns, the community members who came to the mill, people who fished at the small dam when

The Blackburns. *Photo by Sarah Woodward.*

the water was low and the different inceptions of the mill. There were little captions with the history of what was happening, and it made the mill come to life.

The Blackburns were not fancy. They weren't regal. They didn't wear special clothes. The couple looked worn and weathered by the sun and hard work. They looked like most people from the time. If you saw them on the street, you wouldn't think they were anything special. I think that's the beauty of pictures. You get to put faces to names, which gives much more context.

History is one-dimensional without the touch of humanity that photographs bring to a story. Life seemed more simple back in the 1800s, but the needs of the people in the community were relatively the same. What I have learned over the years writing about the histories of different cities in different states is that people are generally predictable. We all have the same wants and needs, and they can be sectioned off into three categories: health, love and money. It doesn't matter the period or the location. Everything involving humans stems from those desires.

I love to bake, so I was taken in by the different selections of flour and mixes. Last year, I tried my hand at making a sourdough starter and failed miserably. I found a package of dehydrated sourdough starter. Intrigued, I looked up the information for the company, and there were step-by-step instructions on how to use the contents in the container. I bought the package, and now, there are two small ramekins of starter, water and flour on my kitchen island. Also, I bought some rye flour to try my hand at baking rye bread in my bread machine.

My sister, who came with me on the trip and took pictures, bought some bourbon-flavored syrup and cornmeal. She said she wanted to make cornbread from scratch. She texted me the next day with pictures of her sausage and jalapeño cornbread. She said it came out really good. The prices for the flour, bread and pancake mixes are a little bit high, but they're also typical for organic products. Plus, there is a kitschy factor to the place. I mean, I will happily tell people my sourdough starter came from the War Eagle Mill. It gives me a good story, and it will make my bread taste that much better—in my mind, anyway.

The second floor of the mill was another part of the store. You get to it by going up a set of small wooden stairs. The floor housed mostly T-shirts and other apparel, books and tin plates. There were some old pieces of wooden furniture that decorated the space. However, the most interesting features of the second floor are the big windows that look over the swelling river. This part of Northwest Arkansas is magical. It's green, lush and feels like nature untouched, even with the farming buildings on the horizon. It's not hard to imagine fairies and gnomes hiding behind rocks and looming in the tall grasses. It has that vibe.

After you walk up another set of stairs, you get to the third floor, which holds a café. It's cute and quaint. It feels like you are in an attic, with its simple open layout and big portrait windows. Everything was made of wood, even the tables. When you walk up the stairs, you immediately run into the counter of the restaurant. There are baked goodies in a case and then a board with the menu.

You put your order in at the counter and sit where you want. The menu was simple. Sandwiches, salads and sides. Sodas and water. Cobbler for dessert. The café is known for its beans and cornbread. However, by the time we made it to the third floor, they were out. I ate lunch with my mom and my sister. We sat at a table right next to one of the big windows. They had chef salads. I had a blackened chicken club sandwich with a side of potato salad and cobbler for dessert. The food was good. The cobbler wasn't too sweet, which is the way I like it.

If you go to the War Eagle Mill, make sure you check out the grounds outside and the giant wheel in the water. There are older parts of the mill lying about, along with other kinds of equipment. There's an old wooden wagon, and sometimes, there is a goat. Its little home is right next to the outhouse restrooms. There are picnic tables outside for sitting and taking in the view.

Also, make sure you take a walk over the bridge. It's wide enough that you can easily walk across even when the cars drive through. On the other side of the bridge, you can visit the Blackburns' two-story home that they built from scratch. Even though it's falling apart and in disrepair, it's still a beautiful piece of architecture.

While I was meandering around War Eagle, watching my sister take pictures for this book, I witnessed an interesting paranormal event. Even though I'm psychic and I usually visit haunted locations, I wasn't in that mode during this trip. War Eagle Mill is known to be haunted. There is no shock that people say it's haunted by Sylvanus Blackburn. He's mostly heard. There are reports of sounds and encounters with poltergeist phenomena. Sometimes, people hear whispered conversations.

Outside, others have seen a man with a long white beard wearing period clothing roaming around. The description resembles those of Blackburn. People have also seen a Confederate soldier wandering around. However, that may not specifically be associated with the mill. There are sightings of soldiers in most of Northwest Arkansas. It's a fairly common phenomenon around here. I had an experience with a soldier that I wrote about in my last book, *Eerie Arkansas*. If you are looking for ghosts, you will probably see a Confederate soldier here. It's par for the course.

And just for the record, when I was in the mill, I didn't feel anything paranormal, but I was more interested in baking at the time. I can see how the building could be haunted, though. With the number of fires on the premises; the wood, which is porous; and the water, which is a conductor, I would be very surprised if there weren't some kind of paranormal phenomena happening there. The place is pretty much a ghost battery, which makes what happened to me make sense.

Like I said before, my sister was taking pictures, and I was meandering. My sister asked me if there was anything of interest we needed to take pictures of before we went into the mill. I looked around and told her no, because the only other thing around that was of interest was the War Eagle Farm, which housed the popular craft fair. There was also the hotel across the street. But I didn't remember reading anything about the hotel, so it wasn't of historical significance.

She looked up at me and asked me where the hotel was. I told her it was the two-story house across the street. I told her that it looked like the hotel is probably a bed-and-breakfast. She said she didn't see a hotel, just an old house. That confused me a bit, because I swear I saw a hotel when we drove over the bridge to get to the mill. And when I walked to the middle of the bridge to look at the river, I saw the sign for the hotel. I even wondered if it was open despite the weird, cold overcast weather.

My sister asked if the hotel had any significance to the mill. I wasn't sure, so I went over the bridge again to check out the sign and to get the details. When I got to the "hotel," I realized it was actually a two-story house. Then when I looked at the sign, it said it was the Blackburn family home. I felt kind of weird about the whole experience, because I like said, I swear I saw the hotel. Yet now, looking at the house, the windows were broken, the back of the house was coming apart and parts of the original foundation were missing. I have no idea how I saw a pristine two-story bed-and-breakfast-type home.

I told my sister that the Blackburns had built the original mill, so the house was very significant. We took pictures. We looked around the outside of the building and acted like tourists. Then we went inside and looked around the store while waiting for my mom so we could have lunch.

I was so intrigued by everything I saw in the wood building that I didn't think much of the confusion with the Blackburn home—until later in the evening, when I was doing the last bit of research about War Eagle. That's

The Blackburns' home. *Photo by Sarah Woodward.*

when I found out the two-story house had, in fact, been a hotel during the 1980s. It was a very popular getaway at the time because of its proximity to the river and its closeness to Rogers. You could feel like you were in the middle of nowhere while also being twenty minutes from a major city. So, you got the best of both worlds.

I think what I experienced is what I call an overlay. That's when the past and the present merge together. In this case, the strongest energy of the hotel overlaid the present energy of the house. The hotel era was the structure's last heyday. So, that's what I saw. Adding that the mill was a ghost battery and the extra water in the river creating more energy, it would make sense that I would be picking up on psychic impressions without even realizing it. I'm notorious for not realizing when the past creeps into present situations. I don't question things until way after the fact. My brain goes with whatever is being presented. Only later do I realize that it didn't make sense. This is the byproduct of being psychic. The past, present and even the future all kind of blend together.

That pretty much sums up War Eagle. It is literally the innovation of the past coloring the present and redefining the future.

PEPPERSAUCE

Rand Hill
Calico Rock, Arkansas, 72519

There aren't many places where you can stand in a modern-day town, turn your head and see a real-life ghost town just down the street.

Nestled along the banks of the White River in North Central Arkansas, Calico Rock is a fully functioning town, with schools, shops and neighborhoods. But on the east side of the bridge lies something very different: a crumbling, time-worn stretch of buildings known as Peppersauce, or East Calico. It's one of the only authentic ghost towns that exists entirely within the city limits of a still-living community.

You don't need to hike for miles to find it. You don't have to squint at maps or dig through overgrowth. It's just there, quiet, empty and weathered by time. A haunting reminder of what was and what didn't last.

If you're interested in seeing it for yourself, the best place to begin is the Calico Rock Museum. They have brochures and walking tour maps you can grab before heading across the bridge to the ghost town. All of the buildings in Peppersauce are privately owned, so you can't go inside, but you can walk along the street and peek through the windows. And honestly, that's often more fun than being allowed inside. The stillness speaks for itself.

The ghost town is made up of about twenty structures, each in a different state of decay. They include a movie theater, a car dealership, a hotel, a funeral home and even an old jail. These aren't cleaned-up tourist versions of a ghost town. They're the real deal—peeling paint, warped wood and sunken doorframes.

This is what happens when time lets go of a place—but not all the way.

Before it was a tourist draw, East Calico was a magnet for the rougher elements of frontier life. In the 1800s, French trappers and traders began settling here, drawn by the White River's accessibility. With them came taverns, makeshift lodging and, eventually, a full-blown river town.

It wasn't long before the area developed a bad reputation. Knife fights and gunfights were common. Sex work was openly practiced. Bootleggers sold a particularly potent moonshine called "peppersauce," named for its fiery kick, in an alley just off the main drag. If you had a problem, you handled it with fists, blades or bullets. The law technically existed—but not in any way that could be called "enforced."

This wasn't a town built on order. It was built on opportunity. And desperation. And liquor. The nickname Peppersauce Alley stuck, and eventually, the entire east side of Calico Rock came to be known by that name. It was the place you went for a good time, but you didn't talk about it.

Like many Arkansas towns, Calico Rock got its boost from the railroad. In 1903, the tracks finally reached the area, transforming it into a critical hub for river and rail trade. Zinc mining, timber and cotton farming became the backbone of the local economy. With the river on one side and the train tracks on the other, East Calico exploded with growth. Businesses lined the waterfront. Boardinghouses popped up. The streets buzzed with workers, travelers, traders and opportunists. It was chaotic, alive and probably smelled like sawdust, tobacco, sweat and whiskey.

By the early twentieth century, Peppersauce had all the makings of a boomtown: hotels to house miners and loggers, shops to sell them boots and tools, and bars to separate them from their wages at the end of the day. But like most boomtowns, it was always living on borrowed time.

The first cracks appeared when cotton began to lose its dominance. Cattle became the more profitable crop, and that shift changed the entire economic makeup of the region. At the same time, the timber industry began to collapse under its own weight. Clear-cutting had stripped the forests, and there was little left to harvest. The jobs dried up. The money stopped coming in.

The train, once the lifeblood of East Calico, ceased stopping there by the 1960s. And if there's one thing that can kill a small town fast, it's the loss of its train service. Floods came through. Fires swept across entire blocks. And just like that, Peppersauce fell into decline. People packed up. Businesses closed. The town shrank—slowly, and then all at once. Usually, that would be the end of a town. Something you read about in books.

But Calico Rock didn't die. It just moved. New development started on higher ground west of Calico Creek. A modern town grew up around the ruins of the old one. And the ghost town was left behind, literally on the edge of the bridge, visible and accessible but disconnected. It didn't vanish. It just got forgotten.

Locals have their own stories about Peppersauce. Some say the old jail is haunted. Others swear they've seen lights flicker in buildings where there's no electricity. The funeral home, naturally, has its own set of eerie tales. And if you ask the right person, they might tell you about the time they heard faint, old-timey piano music coming from the boarded-up hotel late one night.

Whether you believe in ghosts or you don't, it's hard to deny that this place feels different. Maybe it's the sheer weight of history. Maybe it's the absence of sound where you expect there to be life. Or maybe it's something else entirely. But spend enough time in Peppersauce, and you'll start to feel the space between past and present thin out just a little.

What makes Calico Rock and Peppersauce so unique is the way two versions of a town exist side by side. One thriving, one frozen. One still growing, the other collapsing in slow motion. It's a living diorama of Arkansas history: settlement, boom, collapse, reinvention. Most ghost towns get bulldozed, buried under lakes or fenced off for safety. But here, they've just been left. Quietly. Like someone turned off the lights and forgot to come back.

And honestly, that's what makes it worth visiting. It's not commercialized. It's not cleaned up. It hasn't been transformed into a theme park or heritage site. It just is. Raw, real and haunting in a way that feels honest. And for a brief, beautiful moment, you can stand in the middle of a street where the past never quite got the memo that it was over.

PART II

LOST LANDMARKS

MONTE NE

Rogers, Arkansas

The ruins are demolished. You can see the amphitheater, some of the old walls and part of the old bridge in the late fall and winter months, when the lake water levels are low. Go to this website to check the Beaver Lake Water levels: beaver.uslakes.info/Level.asp.

Tucked deep in the Ozark woods, just outside of Rogers, Arkansas, Monte Ne was once a sprawling resort town and wellness destination built on idealism, ambition and a healthy dose of hubris. At its height, it featured two of the largest log structures in the world, Arkansas's first indoor swimming pool and the only presidential convention ever held in the state.

Yet despite a run that spanned over thirty years, Monte Ne was never what anyone would call a smashing success. Overspending, political distraction and an ever-dwindling stream of cash spelled its end. When its founder, William "Coin" Harvey, passed away in 1936, he left behind a failed utopia, a concrete amphitheater to a future that never came and a town that would eventually be swallowed by Beaver Lake.

Long before Monte Ne, Harvey had already made and lost several fortunes. He found early success in real estate and silver mining in Colorado. But what made him a household name in the 1890s was a pamphlet called *Coin's Financial School*, which argued for a free silver economy. He thought unlimited coinage of silver would boost inflation and help debt-ridden farmers and workers. Over two million copies were sold, making it one of the best-selling publications of the time, second only to the Bible.

Monte Ne. *Courtesy of Rogers Historical Center.*

That level of popularity launched Harvey into the national spotlight as one of the country's most vocal monetary reformers. He took the popularity and, in 1895, formed the Patriots of America, a political party focused on direct legislation and silver-backed currency. His party supported Democratic candidate William Jennings Bryan, whose defeat by Republican William McKinley marked the end of Harvey's political ambitions.

Harvey needed a new direction, a new outlet. So, he retreated to the Ozarks because he liked the sprawling green woods and, more importantly, the quiet.

Harvey first purchased five acres near Rogers, Arkansas, while still on the campaign trail. By 1900, he returned to the area and bought an additional 320 acres from a man named Reverend Bailey, who had been living in a rustic log cabin on the property. Harvey moved in and began planning the future.

His son, Tom, was the first to join him and help begin repairs. Eventually, his wife, Anna, and their two other children, Hal and Annette, came to Arkansas, though the reunion was short-lived. A fire tore through the cabin shortly after their arrival, destroying nearly all of Harvey's belongings. Devastated by the loss, Anna and the children returned to Chicago. Anna returned to Arkansas only on rare occasions after that.

But Harvey stayed. He had fallen in love with the wild, untouched beauty of the Ozarks. He once said he appreciated that there were no large cities nearby and few wealthy people. He saw it as a refuge from the status-obsessed political world he had left behind. It was here that his next big dream took root.

THE BIRTH OF MONTE NE

The town originally known as Silver Springs needed a new identity. Harvey renamed it Monte Ne, a name he constructed himself, using *monte* (Spanish for "mountain") and *ne*, which he believed was the Native word for "water." It was a romantic, almost spiritual, rebranding that fit his vision: a health-focused European-style spa town nestled in the natural springs and mountain air of Arkansas.

To begin, he invested heavily in water infrastructure, hiring engineer Albert Graham to dredge canals and redirect the flow of Big Spring and Elixir Spring into a manmade body of water he called Big Spring Lake. He designed charming stonework bridges, wooden walkways and scenic spots for rest and relaxation. Visitors could picnic by the waterfalls, sip the spring water and glide across the water in gondolas or rowboats.

In 1901, Monte Ne officially opened to the public with its first hotel: the three-story Hotel Monte Ne. The building featured two massive wings, each three hundred feet long, with wraparound porches attached to every guest room. The dining room sat on the east end of the structure, while a stairway led directly from the hotel to the lagoon for easy boat access.

For the grand opening, Harvey threw a ball in the dining hall and decorated the exterior with hundreds of Japanese lanterns. He even commissioned a theme song, "Beautiful Monte Ne," written by Edward Wolfe, hoping to brand his creation as a magical place of healing and joy.

Monte Ne riverfront. *Courtesy of Rogers Historical Center.*

Accessibility was key to Harvey's vision. Arkansas was still remote, and he needed a better way for visitors to get to Monte Ne. Cars weren't common yet, so trains were the obvious answer.

Harvey approached city leaders in both Rogers and Lowell, asking for financial backing. Rogers declined, but Lowell invested. The city issued a $250,000 bond to help construct a private five-mile rail line that connected the Monte Ne resort to the main Lowell transfer station.

By June 1902, the train line was operational. Harvey built a rustic train station at the south end of Big Spring Lake, and from there, guests would board gondolas for a ride to the hotel. The trip cost just ten cents, and Harvey promoted the journey as a one-of-a-kind experience. A celebratory opening was held. Though it rained, the festivities went on with a lively dance that lasted well into the early morning hours.

THE HOTELS: MISSOURI ROW AND OKLAHOMA ROW

Harvey envisioned five grand hotels. The first was Missouri Row, completed in 1905. It stretched for four hundred feet and included expansive porches and fireplaces in every room. Rooms were rented for one dollar per night or six dollars per week.

Oklahoma Row followed, though its construction was slower due to funding issues. Built with cement and equipped with electricity, piped-in spring water and a sewer system, Oklahoma Row also featured a large cement tower with a dance hall and dining room. Despite money troubles, it opened in 1909. Rates were $2.40 per day or $10 per week, meals included.

At the time, Oklahoma Row and Missouri Row were among the largest log buildings in the world. They weren't just hotels; they were architectural marvels, standing testaments to Harvey's grand ambitions.

In addition to the hotels, Harvey wanted Monte Ne to have first-class amenities. His family helped construct the state's first indoor swimming pool across from the lagoon. Measuring twenty-five feet wide by fifty feet long, the pool featured both hot and cold water sections, a diving board, dressing rooms and even a small bowling alley.

Fishing and fox hunting were popular pastimes. Harvey made sure the lake was regularly stocked with rainbow trout, and in 1908, Monte Ne hosted the Fox Hunters' Association and its annual hunt, attracting over one hundred participants. He also brought in live music; weekly dances; lawn games, like

Monte Ne, Oklahoma Row postcard. *Courtesy of Rogers Historical Center.*

croquet and lawn tennis; and even Northwest Arkansas's first golf course in 1908. Downtown Monte Ne had its own bank, post office, boutiques and mercantile shops. Harvey created his own local currency, so guests didn't need to carry cash while on vacation.

Despite the excitement, Monte Ne's golden years were brief. Harvey's ambitions were not sustainable to his income. By 1914, the Monte Ne Bank had failed, the railroad was dismantled and his bid for a seat in Congress fell flat. Although the resort still drew visitors, the numbers were never enough to sustain his massive dream.

The Pyramid Project

Harvey became increasingly obsessed with the idea that the world's political and economic systems were destined to collapse. In the 1920s, he pivoted from resort building to doomsday preparation. In his book *Common Sense*, Harvey outlined his belief that society was headed for ruin and proposed a radical solution: a pyramid-shaped time capsule to preserve knowledge for future civilizations.

The capsule's construction began in 1923 on land just south of Big Spring Lake. Harvey envisioned a massive structure containing books, newspapers and records that would explain the fallen world to the survivors of some future disaster. By 1928, he had completed a concrete amphitheater capable of seating up to one thousand people. Although the pyramid itself was never built, the amphitheater served as a platform for speeches and

Monte Ne Amphitheater. *Courtesy of Rogers Historical Center.*

concerts. Inspired by the Egyptian craze of the era, Harvey charged curious visitors twenty-five cents to view the construction and listen to him wax philosophical about the coming apocalypse. At its peak, the amphitheater drew over twenty thousand visitors in just four months.

In 1930, Harvey founded the Liberty Party and launched one final political campaign. His platform was detailed in *The Book*, which attendees were required to read to participate in his presidential convention, the only one ever held in Arkansas. About 786 delegates showed up, far fewer than the thousands he had hoped for. Harvey ultimately came in fifth in the 1932 presidential election, losing to Franklin D. Roosevelt. Though he was politically sidelined, Harvey continued to write and publish under the *Liberty Bell* newsletter, railing against the Roosevelt administration and trying to keep the flame of his vision alive.

By the mid-1930s, Harvey's health was failing. Nearly blind and suffering from various ailments, he died in Monte Ne on February 11, 1936, at the age of eighty-four. A death mask was made of his face, and today, it's preserved at the Rogers Historical Museum.

After Harvey's death, Monte Ne faded into obscurity. The hotels changed hands multiple times and were used intermittently for lodging and local events. But the era of grand openings and gondola rides was over.

When Beaver Lake was created in the 1960s, much of Monte Ne was flooded. Today, during low water levels, parts of the old amphitheater and submerged structures emerge like concrete memories of one man's wild, beautiful and ultimately doomed dream.

MONTE NE HAS BEEN TORN DOWN AND WASHED AWAY

In December 2022, I went to Monte Ne for the first time. I was visiting someone I met online who lived near Beaver Lake. I had brunch with her and a girlfriend. She invited us to her house afterward, and we had a strange conversation. I don't know how or why we ended up talking about Monte Ne, but I truly believe that I met this person just so I could experience the ruins.

She told me about the tower that still stood just off the lake. She said that sometimes, when it rains, the first floor floods. However, for the most part, you can go there and investigate. I am super curious and asked her and my friend if they wanted to go on a little adventure to go see the ruins. My friend was up for it, but this new person didn't want to leave her house. Then it started to rain, which nixed the idea all together.

Sort of.

I couldn't get the idea of Monte Ne out of my head. There was something about the energy of the place that had my intuition tingling. I'm still not sure why. So, even though everyone had left and gone their own way, I decided to Google "Monte Ne Ruins" to see where I was in relationship to the destination. It's strange that its location is marked on Google Maps. I was only fifteen minutes away. Even though it was raining hard, I took this as a sign to go on a little side quest before I went home.

Monte Ne Tower ruins. *Photo by author.*

I went down some backroads through some twists and turns and then finally landed on a straight highway on the outer edges of Rogers. My phone directions took me straight to a parking area that I assumed went to the ruins. The rain was falling heavily when I got out of the car, and I stepped into an ankle-deep puddle. Luckily, I was wearing boots that day, but I still felt the squish of water moving into my socks. The area was overgrown, thick with high grass, weeds and shrubbery. I followed a craggy cement path with puddles in the cracks. The rain left streaks on my glasses as I looked for anything that resembled the remnants of Monte Ne.

As I went around the corner, I saw the three-story tower behind a slanted fence. As I walked toward it, I realized that the base of the cement structure was partly underwater. Once I got to the fence, I noticed an opening. I slipped through it and looked around. The tower had been painted with graffiti from top to bottom. Various colors and primitive scribbling decorated the cement structure. There were no windows or doors. It was basically an empty hull.

I couldn't get into the building because the water level was rising, and the rain was making it hard for me to see. Still, I tried to look around as much as possible because of my curiosity. There was something about the spirit of the place. It held a magic that I still don't understand. It felt powerful for whatever reason. Maybe it was the lake rising. Maybe it was the rain. Maybe it was the chaotic energy of the incoming storm. But the ruins felt kinetic and liminal. It felt alive.

I knew after that experience that I had to go back to the ruins—but not before I did some research. I went down a rabbit hole and learned as much as I could. My friend Kelly knew a lot about Monte Ne because she had grown up in the area. She said that the cement path I was walking on was actually the foundation for one of the hotels. When the lake rose from the spring rains, her family would bring their kayaks and lift off from the cement slabs. She also told me that there were parts of some of the rooms from the hotel that I was standing on and didn't realize it.

After doing some more research, I found out that the tower and the cement base were part of the Oklahoma Row portion of Monte Ne. In its time, it was very elite, with all of the most luxurious amenities. It used to have exterior stairs that went up to the other stories. However, they had broken down and were demolished long ago.

A few weeks passed. The holidays came and went. Kelly told me that when the lake gets low, you can see parts of the amphitheater that are usually underwater. She kept an eye on the weather and the lake levels. Then one day, she texted me and told me that the lake was at the lower levels, and she said we should go see if we could see that top of the round stone structure.

Of course, I wanted to go again. So, we met up and headed out to the ruins. She showed me how to go past the tower and turn the corner to get to the bottom rooms. Most of the time, they were underwater, but during the colder months, they were in full view. Walking through them, you could see the grit and sediment sticking everywhere since the structure had been underwater for

Top: Monte Ne, Oklahoma Row ruins. *Photo by author.*

Bottom: The top of the Monte Ne Amphitheater under Beaver Lake. *Photo by author.*

so long. Some the rooms looked like old closets or part of the basement. And others seemed like they were some kind of living area or maybe lounge area. It had a fireplace, and it seemed larger than the other rooms.

Once we toured the lower rooms, we walked around the peninsula of the tower, and Kelly showed me the other side of the Monte Ne Ruins, which housed the foundation, chimney and brick pieces of the Missouri Row hotels. I was surprised that it was all there right in plain sight, but I hadn't ventured far enough to see it.

After our adventure through the hotel remnants, we drove to the other side of the lake, where it's easier to see the top of the amphitheater through the water. We got a picture of what we saw and then visited William "Coin" Harvey's grave site, which sits on a little plot of private property in a residential area.

I thought that maybe going back to the Monte Ruins would change the way I felt about the area. But just the opposite happened. I felt more connected to it. I felt the excitement of it. I went back a few more times until February 2023, when the City of Rogers decided to tear it down because it was seen as a hazard. Kelly and I visited the ruins the day before the demolition. To my surprise, we weren't the only ones who came to give their reverence. There were slews of people who came to say their goodbyes. They talked about their memories of the ruins.

It was almost like a funeral for a time that had been forgotten. So many people had these sweet stories of playing in the ruins as children. Attaching a rope to the second story of the tower and swinging into the lake. Going to the ruins with friends as teenagers to drink and create mischief.

While we were reminiscing with these lovely people, I couldn't help thinking about Mr. Harvey. He had a dream, and he birthed it into being with sheer tenacity. With sheer will. He didn't give up on what he wanted, and for a time, Monte Ne was a haven. A little piece of heaven on earth, and Harvey was the master of ceremonies. I think the townspeople picked up on that energy. They went there to bathe in the energy of all the good times, and they created their own memories. It all became intertwined. The past breathing into the future giving it a wonderous life.

In December 2024, I visited the Monte Ne Ruins one last time. I wanted to see what it was like after the demolition. I wanted to know if the spirit of the place had changed. It had. It was empty. It felt hollow. The tower was gone. The cement landing was gone. The lower rooms were gone. All that was left was dirt and piles of broken concrete from the demolition.

It was weird and sad. The place felt stripped of its magic.

The chimney from the Missouri Row still stood. The foundation and the brick walls were still there. But a tree had fallen on top of the concrete wall. There were more weeds and shrubbery than usual. It felt abandoned and displaced. Everything about the place was wrong. The joy had been stripped from the air. It felt barren.

It felt like, when the tower was demolished, the memories and the good times went with it. It transformed the hope and good memories into dust. There was nothing left. I've never experienced something like that before. Usually, the energy of a place stays even without the buildings being there. But I truly feel there was something special about the tower. I think it was like a talisman for the land. I think it protected the space, and it held the memories within its walls.

The land and lake in that area will never be the same. I don't think I will ever go back again. I don't want to taint my memories of the place with the reality of what it has become. It is the place of the lost and the forgotten. People talk about the place fondly, but nobody will ever experience it again. It is now a piece of folklore that will live on in the mythology of Northwest Arkansas.

Remnants of Oklahoma Row. *Photo by author.*

I am grateful for my time at Monte Ne. Thank you, William Harvey, for creating your dream and letting me share a small part of it. We will be connected by the dream and vision of the happy memories that were created beyond time and space. We never met, but you will live in the hearts of all of those who got to be a part of your legacy.

DINOSAUR WORLD

8608 Highway 187
Eureka Springs, Arkansas 72631

While Dinosaur World is now permanently closed, you can still see part of the park from the side of the road. Many of the dinosaurs are still visible. You can also drive up to the original entrance and look through the fence and barricade. Please do not trespass.

Dinosaur World was a thriving theme park that housed over one hundred life-size statues of dinosaurs, cavemen and prehistoric creatures. Originally called Farwell's Dinosaur Park, it opened its doors in 1967 to travelers visiting Beaver Lake. The park said it was "out in the middle of nowhere," because it covered over sixty-five acres of the Ozark National Forest, just outside of Eureka Springs, Arkansas.

Dinosaur World was the brainchild of Ola Farwell, who hired Emmet Sullivan to design six to ten life-size dinosaur statues for his new park. Sullivan helped sculpt the profiles on Mount Rushmore and is known for the sixty-seven-foot-tall *Christ of Ozarks* statue that stands on Magnetic Mountain in the Passion Play theme park in Eureka Springs. Locals A.C. McBride and Orvis Parker oversaw the actual construction of the dinosaurs. McBride had been the chief mortar artist on the *Christ of Ozarks* project, and Parker was a local evangelist.

Eventually, the number of dinosaurs grew to the point where it became the largest dinosaur theme park in the world. Dinosaur World was open from 7:00 a.m. to 7:00 p.m. Admission was one dollar for adults and fifty

Above: King Kong from Dinosaur World. *Public domain.*

Left: A current picture of one of the dilapidated dinosaurs in what's left of Dinosaur World. *Photo by Sarah Woodward.*

cents for children under six. Farwell stated that during his ownership, his family never lost money on the park.

In the late 1970s, the park was sold to Ken Childs. He changed its name to John Agar's Land of Kong and added a forty-foot statue of King Kong. Actor John Agar let Child use his name in the name of the park because he had starred in the 1976 remake of the *King Kong* movie. He famously married Shirely Temple when she was seventeen years old. They had one child together but then divorced because of his drinking problems. His career suffered from his drinking as well. In many articles, its stated that Agar owned a portion of the business. However, he only lent his name. He had no financial affiliation to the theme park.

Sometime in the 1980s, the name of the park was changed to Dinosaur World. In 2005, the theme park closed its doors, leaving everything as it was. The gift shop that was painted with the world's largest Noah's Ark mural still had full shelves of memorabilia. Unfortunately, in 2011, the gift shop burned down, and the building no longer stands.

Most of the dinosaurs and cavemen are still at the park. As you drive down the road toward Beaver Lake, you can spot the statues through dense foliage. The swinging bridge that goes across a small water feature still stands.

The park is now private property and fenced off. You can park on the side of the road to get a glimpse of what used to be, or you can drive up to the old entrance that is now barricaded. Just make sure you don't trespass.

ARE THOSE DINOSAURS?

I'm originally from a bedroom community beach town nestled between Hollywood and Santa Barbara. I didn't leave the area until my mid-thirties, when I headed east to the flat, dusty desert of Tucson, Arizona. Being a water sign in a place as dry and brittle as the desert was a challenge for me. I stayed in the area for nearly eight years, but the transitional nature of the desert got to me, and I wanted to be in a lush environment again. I needed to be near the water. So, I ended up in Northwest Arkansas, where my mother owned a home in Eureka Springs.

I knew nothing about Arkansas or its rich history. It felt weird to be in the woods all the time, but there were lakes everywhere. There was moisture in the air. And the spirit of place buzzed with the energy of something ancient and powerful.

When I'm in a new area, one of my favorite things to do is get lost on purpose. Find hidden roads and check out sights that I have never seen before. On one of these adventures, I ended up going down the road that takes you to Beaver Dam. I found out there is a swimming section of the lake in that area, and it quickly became one of my favorite spots for summer picnics. Despite the sweltering heat, I loved barbecuing near the water and going for a swim when the heat became too unbearable.

Sometimes, when I was in a thinking mood, I would drive down to the dam and park. Being near the water helped me get my head on straight. It was on one of these drives that I accidentally discovered Dinosaur World. I had driven down that stretch of highway a bunch of times and never really noticed anything peeking out from the trees. But for some reason, on this one day, I was really noticing my surroundings.

From just outside of my periphery, I swear I saw a dinosaur. Confused, I looked to my right to make sure I wasn't completely losing my mind, and as

I drove by, I saw part of another dinosaur poking out from the shrubbery. As I kept driving and turning my head, I saw a partial structure that looked like a swinging bridge.

Confused, I turned my car around and drove slower this time to make sure what I was seeing was real. I even parked my car and walked down the side of the road. That's when I realized that there were dinosaurs everywhere. Plus, there were other strange things like a giant tarantula. And yes, I saw a swinging bridge. I took a lot of pictures. Then I drove around looking for an entrance. I found the opening where the entrance should be with a haphazard sign that said, "Dinosaur World." That's when I started doing research, and to my dismay, I found out that it was a relic—and there was no way I could go into the area to check out all the dinosaurs.

Every time I go down that road, I always look for the heads of the giant dinosaurs peeking out from the giant woods. Every time, it makes me smile. It brings me a little bit of joy. Even though it's closed, it's still worth the drive, just to experience a little piece of cool Arkansian history.

DOGPATCH USA

9467 State Highway 7
Marble Falls, Arkansas 72648

Dogpatch USA, now permanently closed, was a theme park on Highway 7, located between the cities of Harrisson and Jasper. The park was based on a comic strip called *Lil' Abner*, created by cartoonist Al Capp. The comic strip was set in the fictional town of Dogpatch, hence the name of the park.

In 1966, Albery Raney Sr. decided to sell his family trout farm and listed it with Harrisson real estate agent O.J. Snow. The realtor looked at the property and envisioned a pioneer-themed amusement park. It was an idea that he had thrown around for years, and he had finally found the right property to make his dream a reality.

Snow and a group of investors put together Recreational Enterprises, Incorporated (REI), to start developing the land and pitch the idea to Capp. Home videos and attraction descriptions were sent to the cartoonist for review. The proposal suggested train rides, paddles boats, horseback rides, a shop with local arts and crafts and a fudge shop. Other suggestions were an apiary, a honey hut, a botanical garden, family-themed presentations, rustic-themed presentations and *Lil' Abner* characters that would roam the park.

Snow promised Capp that the park wouldn't have any loud attractions, like roller coasters or thrill rides, because it would mess with the rustic vibe of the Ozark woods. Capp said he initially took this offer seriously because he had once driven through the area and thought it would be the perfect

Old postcard of Dogpatch USA. *Public domain.*

setting for his imaginary town. On January 4, 1967, Capp accepted the offer for Dogpatch USA and gave REI the rights to his characters.

At first, the news of a *Lil' Abner* theme park was met with skepticism. Arkansas officials and townspeople were afraid that the comic strip–related park would further the "hillbilly" stereotype. Officials were asked about their opinions on the attraction. There was a consensus that other parks had been built in the area, and none of them had the Disneyland success that was needed in order to thrive and survive. Plus, some thought the property values around the park might go down, which would cause issues in the housing market. Despite these reservations, the Publicity and Parks Commission toured the property and approved the plans for the park. Then Harrison Commerce put its stamp of approval on the plans.

On October 3, 1967, Al Capp and his wife attended the groundbreaking ceremony for the Dogpatch USA amusement park. The initial buildings and rides cost around $1.3 million to construct. There were plans to build an RV park, an amphitheater, a collection of motels and a golf course, but they were never fully realized.

The property housed a cavern called Mystic Caverns. It was officially renamed Dogpatch Cavern and renovated for safety issues. New walkways, rails and lighting were put in the cave to accommodate patrons. While bulldozing the initial cavern, the builders found an entrance to a second cavern. The second entrance was blocked off to keep it pristine. The cave was named Old Man Moses Cave, and the idea was to put it on the list of things that would be worked on while the second phase of building began.

Traditional wood cabins from the Ozark Mountains were dismantled, shipped to the amusement park property and then reassembled. An 1834 watermill was restored and made to be fully functional. The investors wanted to make the theme park experience as rustic as possible. On May 17, 1968,

Dogpatch USA opened its doors to over eight thousand visitors. A statue of Jubilation T. Cornpone was unveiled in the middle of the town during Capp's dedication speech. A crowd of about two thousand people attended the event.

Attendance fees for the park were $1.50 for adults and $0.75 for kids. During the 1968 season, the park made a net profit of around $100,000. Attendance was better than expected, and a Los Angeles consulting firm projected around 400,000 visitors the first year and then over 1.2 million in the first ten years. They also projected over $5 million in net profit.

However, Dogpatch USA had only 300,000 attendees in 1968 and around 200,000 attendees the next year. There is speculation that there may have been more visitors than previously recorded. In a 1997 article from the *Arkansas Democrat-Gazette*, it is said that the park never reported any more than 200,000 visitors per year. However, in the same newspaper, an article six months later said that the park had almost 1 million attendees a year. Nobody knows what the actual number was for attendance, but the park did have a degree of success overall.

In 1969, there was a disagreement between the investors of REI. Snow wanted to put all profits back into the theme park, while other investors wanted to split the profits among themselves. A man named Jess Odom bought up most of the shares of the amusement park for $750,000 and gained a controlling interest in the park. He was expected to invest $5 million to $7 million in renovations to the amusement park. He signed a licensing agreement with Capp to use the likeness and jargon of all the *Lil' Abner* cartoon characters until 1998. Odom was also expected to receive 2 to 3 percent of ticket sales.

By 1972, the park was a huge success, and Odom had the idea to create a second theme park called Marble Falls, which would be the sister attraction to Dogpatch USA. He bought up the rest of the shares from REI for around $700,000 so he could start his expansion. The idea was to have two parks that would be ideal for tourists to visit year round. The second park would have a winter theme with a toboggan run, an ice rink, a ski area and a convention center. He wanted to have the second amusement park ready by Christmas that same year.

In 1973, interest rates skyrocketed, and there was an energy crisis that kept people at home. Many could not afford to travel to tourist locations anymore. Many of the rustic- or hillbilly-themed TV shows were phased out during this period. It seemed people were looking for a new kind of entertainment.

Many of Capp's projects faltered. The restaurant chain was never built. A pilot for the *Lil' Abner* TV show was produced and aired on ABC but had poor reviews. It was canned and never picked up for a series. Park attendance started to dwindle. The mild Arkansas winters did not help the sales of the snow-themed Marble Falls sister theme park. Odom was losing money. He was already $2 million in debt, but he borrowed another $1.5 million to stay afloat.

In 1974, Odom partnered with the University of Arkansas to create an in-park repertory theater to bring in more visitors. The troupe planned to do five well-known plays and then tour with two new plays during the off season. The theater was a big disappointment and delivered only two of its planned five plays because of bad turnout. While the troupe did not return to the theater for any future seasons, it is still active at the University of Arkansas.

In 1976, the Union Planters Bank started foreclosure proceedings on the park's $3.5 million in debt. In 1977, Capp decided to retire, and the comic series ended with the end of his career. Without the *Lil' Abner* comic, there was no real motivation for people to go to the theme park. That same year, First National Bank of Arkansas started foreclosure proceedings on his $600,000 of debt. The Marble Falls ski resort was closed permanently, as Odom claimed that he had lost $50,000 to $100,000 a year while it was open.

In 1979, two personal injury lawsuits were filed against Dogpatch USA for $200,000 in compensation. The lawsuits were settled a year later. The overhead costs were outweighing the profits, and Odom tried to have the towns of Harrisson and Jasper issue tourism bonds to refinance the theme park. Odom's efforts proved to be unsuccessful, and he shifted gears. He was in talks with a company called God's Path Inc. to sell the property and create a biblical-themed amusement park. However, the funding for the project never materialized.

The heatwave of 1980 tanked sales. This was the end for the failing business. In October that same year, the Union Planters Bank took possession of the property. A month later, Dogpatch USA filed for bankruptcy. The property was put up for sale to accommodate $7 million dollars' worth of loans.

In 1981, OEI bought Dogpatch USA for an undisclosed amount. The general manager, Wayne Thompson, cut the staff by 50 percent and diversified the attractions, including adding another roller coaster. The amphitheater held music concerts, like those of Reba McIntyre and Ike and Tina Turner. Thompson also brought in sponsors, like Coca-Cola and Tyson, and added other characters to the park like Spider-Man, Batman and Robin. He hired Denver Pyle (Uncle Jess from the *Dukes of Hazard*) to be the spokesman for Dogpatch USA and had him appear in television commercials for the park. Thompson's marketing tactics worked, and during the five years he was manager, visitors spent more money per person than any other year when the park was open.

The Dogpatch Cavern and Old Man Moses Cave were sold to Bruce Raney, who renovated them and changed their names to Mystic Caverns and Crystal Domes to make them their own tourist attractions. Raney owned the caves for three years, and then in 1984, he sold them to Omni Properties. The twin caves are still operating as tourist attractions today.

Marble Falls was mired in confusing and legal problems. It was unclear who actually owned that part of the property. By 1984, Odom, under the name Buffalo River Resorts, sold parcels of land for timeshares and condominiums. There were issues with the sales because there were liens on the property. In court, Odum, was able to get an exception that said he could sell as long as he was transparent about the financial instability of the property.

In 1987, The Entertainment and Leisure Corporation (Telcor) bought 90 percent of the Dogpatch USA shares. The remaining 10 percent stayed with OEI. Telcor managed two other parks in Michigan and Hot Springs, Arkansas. In 1988, Thompson stepped down as general manager of the park. Lynn Spradley took over and managed Dogpatch USA until 1991. During his tenure, he complained that the park had to do too much marketing just to get people to visit. He also said most kids didn't even know who Lil' Abner was because the comic book had been out of print for at least ten years.

Attendance started to dwindle, because in the late 1980s, Silver Dollar City in Branson had similar attractions on a grander scale. In Mountain View, there was the Ozark Folk Center, which was a fully subsidized park. These newer parks were not associated with an outdated cartoon franchise, which made them more approachable.

In 1991, due to financial problems, the park was scaled down to an arts and crafts theme. The *Lil' Abner* theme was completely nixed, and there was no general admission. Patrons paid per attraction.

Dogpatch USA was permanently closed on October 14, 1993.

THE WEIRDNESS OF DOGPATCH USA

Sometime around late 2019, I was invited to do a paranormal investigation and hang out at the Dogpatch USA site. My mom's boyfriend at the time knew the owner, and they would consistently go to the property to camp, hang out and hold events. At the time, I lived only about an hour away, and I thought it would be a cool adventure. However, the weekend I was supposed to go, I got a weird feeling about the whole situation and, at the last minute, decided to stay home instead.

I am not one to give up on an adventure, but I do trust my intuition, especially when it comes to visiting a location out in the middle of the woods. I talked about it with my mom later, and she said she understood why I had the weird feeling. She had been to the property a handful of times and said the whole area has a strange feeling about it. She said that the land might be cursed. She said there were rumors. Hearing this bit of information, I don't regret not going.

According to the folklore around these parts, the land was once inhabited by a Native tribe. There are a few different versions of this story, but the one

Abandoned waterslide at Dogpatch USA. *Public domain.*

that I have heard the most says that the chief of this Native tribe sold the land to some white people, knowing that it was tainted. Since that transaction, the land has been cursed, and anything on it will automatically fail or go bad. I don't know if the tale is real. The Shawnee lived in the area and could have made some kind of crazy deal with a settler. This wasn't unheard of, but there's no documentation to prove that it happened. I think that's why it's so unnerving. The history of the place is so open ended.

The Dogpatch site is supposedly haunted, but there's not a lot of information on that either. I found a few videos mentioning the paranormal phenomenon, but it's the regular fare: footsteps, disembodied voices, the sounds of people talking and a man in overalls and a white beard wandering around the premises. (All the same things at the War Eagle Mill, minus the typical Confederate soldier.)

My mom said she never experienced anything paranormal. It was more of a feeling, she said. She just didn't like the way the woods made her feel. Her boyfriend at the time felt that it was haunted and said that he had heard things and felt things that were unexplainable. It didn't stop him going out to the property, but it did unnerve him a bit. He always felt like he was being watched.

There's one more story that people talk about if you ask about Dogpatch USA, and it's a weird one. I've heard two versions of this story, and I have not been able to find how it became part of the area's folklore. Both versions start with a man who was riding on his motorcycle on the property. Apparently, it's important that the man had permission to be there. People make a big deal about making sure that detail is not overlooked.

Anyway, this guy rode through the property and did not see a wire line hanging from two posts. In the first version, that man rode between the posts and decapitated himself. His ghost lurks around the site, and sometimes, people see his head on the ground or hear his motorcycle, even though there's no one there.

The second version is even more strange. The man still rides through the wire and almost decapitates himself. But in this tale, he then sues the owner of the property for not putting up a sign or making the wire more visible. The two men go to court, and the judge rules in favor of the man. He was supposed to get a large sum of money for this tragedy. However, the owner didn't have the money. So, the man went back to court and was given the deed of Dogpatch USA as his compensation.

I've gone through the history of every owner of the property. I have not found anything that resembles this story, but it doesn't matter. The story lives on, and if you even mention Dogpatch, that's the first thing you will hear: "Did you hear about the guy that got decapitated?"

Let the tale live on.

WHAT'S NEXT FOR DOGPATCH USA?

In 2020, Johnny Morris, the founder and CEO of Bass Pro Shops bought the property for $1.2 million. There's not a lot of information about what is going on with the site. Most of the articles I found were from 2020 and 2021. I did find a 2023 article from *Arkansas Money and Politics* (*AMP*) and here's what it said:

> *Initially, plans for a Morris-developed attraction at Dogpatch called Marble Falls Nature Park, which would look like Morris' Dogwood Canyon Nature Park in southern Missouri, were revealed, but nothing ever materialized.*
>
> *Debbie Bennett, president of hospitality at Bass Pro, told* AMP *there are no solid plans for the property currently, but her group may soon conduct another on-site visit, she said.*
>
> *With conservation in mind, Bennett said there remains a lot of cleanup to do on the property in addition to environmental hurdles to clear regarding Mill Creek and the cavern.*

Essentially, there's not a lot going on with the property. Could it be the curse up on the land taking its toll? Or did Morris just buy a piece of property on a whim and forget what to do with it? I wonder if he's heard about the decapitated guy.

I guess time will tell.

ARKANSAS TUBERCULOSIS SANATORIUM

256 Carey Road
Booneville, Arkansas 72927-6511

If you drive just south of Booneville and let your instincts take the wheel, you'll eventually find yourself climbing Sanatorium Hill. The view encompasses breathtaking rolling hills, scattered trees and sky that seems to stretch just a little wider up here. But it's not just the elevation that'll steal your breath.

It's the history.

You might not know what this place is at first glance. The buildings still stand, many of them weathered but intact. It's too big to be a school, too quiet to be a hospital, too orderly to be a ghost town. This was the Arkansas Tuberculosis Sanatorium, one of the largest and most successful institutions of its kind in the country. For more than sixty years, it was the final stop for tens of thousands of Arkansans with tuberculosis, or the "white plague," which swept across the world in suffocating waves. From its opening in 1909 to its closure in 1973, the hill was home to pain, hope, experimentation, grief and resilience.

To understand the scale of the sanatorium, you have to understand what tuberculosis (TB) was before antibiotics. It wasn't just a cough. It was a death sentence. A slow, wasting disease that chewed through your lungs, your bones and, eventually, your dignity. In the early 1900s, Arkansas had one of the highest rates of tuberculosis in the country, and medical science was still scrambling to figure out what worked to treat it.

Booneville Sanatorium. *Public domain.*

There were no miracle drugs. Just theories. The remedy for tuberculosis at the time was rest, clean air and isolation. So, the state carved out eight hundred acres on this hill outside Booneville and decided to build a self-sustaining, structured community where those with TB could live and hopefully get better while not infecting anyone else.

It had its own laundry, dairy, chapel, fire department, telephone system and staff quarters. There was even a recreation hall. At its peak, the sanatorium's combined population of patients and staff was larger than that of Booneville itself.

Its oldest structure is an Art Deco–style administration building that went up in 1909. In 1941, a building was named after Leo Nyberg, a former patient who survived TB and later became a state legislator. The Nyberg Building is massive, covering 140,000 square feet and stretching for a tenth of a mile, with floor after floor of patient rooms, treatment areas and clinical space. It was considered a monument to medicine.

But despite the institution's ambition, its atmosphere inside was bleak. It had cold tiles, long halls, echoing ceilings. Everything about it was designed for cleanliness, not comfort. Survivors often describe it as sterile and mechanical. It was less like a hospital and more like a holding facility.

Children were kept on separate floors, often for months or years at a time. Families couldn't visit freely. Some patients arrived as teenagers and left as adults. Some didn't leave at all. One man said the building reminded him of Arkham Asylum from the *Batman* series.

Richard Myers, a former patient, once described life there by saying, "Every day was a Tuesday."

Meaning it was monotonous, quiet and uneventful. A blur of sameness and silence. Days passed without milestones. Birthdays and holidays were forgotten. Even seasons lost their reality when you couldn't leave your bed or your room. There was no internet. No TikTok. No phones, unless you were lucky or well-off. Entertainment meant books, radios or, if you were feeling ambitious, watching the birds out your window. There were no shared meals, no casual walks outside. The focus was rest. Total, uninterrupted, soul-numbing rest.

Nurses would sometimes sneak in small comforts. One woman recalled the joy of being brought a hamburger from Booneville—something warm and greasy and forbidden. That one burger, years later, still meant something. In a place built for survival, little moments like that became everything.

But not everyone made it out. In fact, most didn't. During the institution's early years, the mortality rate was over 70 percent. Even when treatments improved, it was still a dangerous place to be. The staff tried their best to shield patients from the realities of death. When someone passed away, nurses would close every door down the hallway before rolling the gurney through. The patients learned to count the doors. They'd hear the slams, one after another. If the sequence skipped a room, they knew who had died. And then came the wheels and the slow squeaky sounds of the gurney.

THE EXPERIMENTAL TREATMENTS

Many of the treatments were theoretical and tested on the patients. Most were brutal and could even be considered cruel. In one procedure, doctors would collapse a lung to "let it rest." This involved lifting a patient's arm, deflating their lung and then inserting ping-pong balls or other inert materials into the chest cavity. The goal was to stop the diseased lung from working, under the theory that this would help it heal.

There were surgical options, too. Ribs were removed to allow the chest wall to cave in, known as thoracoplasty. Spinal fusions, bronchoscopy experiments, high-dose X-rays, all of it done in the name of science, with limited tools and even more limited understanding.

Even with these crude treatments, the Booneville Sanatorium became known as one of the most advanced and effective TB hospitals in the world. By the 1960s, its death rate had dropped below 10 percent. Medicine had caught up—but not before leaving thousands of stories in its wake. Some of the most heartbreaking stories come from the youngest patients. There were kids who didn't understand what was happening to them, only that they were being taken away. Many were too sick to fight. Others arrived with a parent, only to be separated on arrival. Some never saw their families again.

These children grew up in isolation. They missed school. They missed home. Some healed and were discharged. Others simply faded into the system. The trauma of that kind of removal doesn't vanish when the lungs clear. It lingers. Many survivors struggled with depression, PTSD and long-term trust issues. Some still can't talk about it without crying.

THE TOWN WITH THE TOWN

The sanatorium wasn't just a hospital. It was a fully operational town. Staff lived on site. There were dances, choir rehearsals, card games, church services. People fell in love here. They got married. They got divorced. They waited for letters, for test results, for God, for hope.

It wasn't uncommon for patients to remain here for years, even after recovery, because going home wasn't simple. There were still fears about contagions. The stigma was real. TB marked you. So, people stayed. They made lives out of fragments. They made the best of what they had.

As progressive as the facility was for its time, it was also a product of its time. The Booneville Sanatorium was a whites-only institution for most of its operation. Black patients were sent to a much smaller, less-equipped facility in Alexander, Arkansas, known simply as the Negro Sanatorium. Racism shaped access to care, quality of treatment and the outcomes for countless Arkansans. The Booneville Sanatorium might have been world-renowned, but it wasn't equal.

In the mid-twentieth century, antibiotic breakthroughs changed everything. TB was no longer a mystery. It was treatable with drugs like streptomycin and isoniazid. Hospitalizations dropped. Outpatient care became the norm. Booneville began to empty. By 1973, the sanatorium officially closed. The patients were discharged. The beds were stripped. The staff dispersed. That part of the chapter closed.

The facility was then repurposed as the Booneville Human Development Center, a residential care center for adults with developmental disabilities. It is still operating today, but many of the original buildings are unused. Some are preserved. Others stand as silent reminders of what was.

GHOSTS AND ECHOES

With a place like this, you know the ghost stories are coming. Visitors report strange sounds like footsteps in empty halls, whispers through closed doors, cold spots on warm days. Some say they can hear the squeaky sounds of the gurney rolling through the hallways. Others hear doors slamming down long corridors, just like they used to do when someone passed.

The Booneville Sanatorium isn't just a medical relic. It's a mirror. It shows us who we were when we didn't have the answers. It reveals the sacrifices made in the name of health. It reminds us how fear can isolate and how hope can persist in the bleakest places.

It also challenges us to remember the people, not just the stats. The institution's seventy thousand patients weren't numbers. They were people with names and dreams and stories. This chapter is for them.

SANATORIUM HILL

I live two hours away from Booneville and previously knew nothing about the town or its history. That happens a lot. I live in a tiny little post stamp of a town surrounded by the Ozarks. My neighborhood is literally cut out of the forest. There are a lot of little communities out here like that, and Booneville is one of them. It's small, home to mostly grassy flatland and farmhouses, old buildings and too many churches.

I never would have known about Booneville if my friend Stephanie had not gone house hunting and found a big property on the outskirts of the city. She used it as an excuse to visit me and go on a road trip. The whole experience was weird and kind of off. I can laugh about it now, but at the time, we were both side eyeing every aspect of our time on Sanatorium Hill.

On the day of our trip, we woke up early and went out to breakfast. Did I mention I live in the Ozarks? People think I'm exaggerating. If you go twenty minutes outside of my city, it's dense forest. I'm talking about hairpin turns covered by a blanket of tree branches and leaves. People come out here to camp and search for our version of Bigfoot. It's that kind of dense.

I'm not a nature person. I don't like camping. I don't like mountains. I especially don't like hairpin turns because I'm prone to car sickness. Sometimes it hits me, and sometimes it doesn't. But on this day, my equilibrium was not having any of it, and I puked up all my breakfast on the side of the road. Stephanie promised we would find an easier route home. I laughed it off and trekked on.

I have no idea how I found out about the Booneville Sanatorium. I think it was curiosity and Google, because whenever Stephanie and I are together, weird things happen. We tend to accidentally end up in weird paranormal situations. I am pretty sure I was trying to get ahead of the curve this time.

We got to Booneville early and decided to check out the sanatorium property. There's a museum on the premises, and at the time, the website said that it gave paranormal tours. So, we decided to look for the museum

Top: Booneville Sanatorium, 2023. *Photo by author.*

Bottom: Booneville Sanatorium, administrative building. *Photo by author.*

and hopefully get some more information. First off, I was not prepared for the breadth of the compound. It's not just a sanatorium building. It's like an entire city within a city. There were buildings on buildings on buildings. Then on the outskirts, there were older houses. It's so big it should have its own zip code.

We had no idea where we were going, so we drove around and found an administrative building. However, it was closed, so we drove around some more, looking for anything that resembled a museum. We found the little museum building and realized it was closed that day. We headed to the large sanatorium building, hoping there would be an administrative section that was still being used. Maybe someone in the office would know about the tours. Or maybe we could just look inside that day with permission.

The sanatorium building is massive. You don't realize just how big it is until you are right up in front it. The building is four stories of brick, with dark windows and a strange sense of darkness. It felt lonely, vast and haunted. You don't have to go in to know that there is strange energy emanating from this behemoth.

Our driving around the area was noticed, and someone came up to us to ask what we needed. We explained we were looking for someone to talk to about the museum and to get a tour. We were told to go to an administrative building on the hill above the official sanatorium building.

We talked to a few people, but nobody knew what we could do to get a tour. People were called, and then finally, someone got permission to let us in and look around. But there were keys that needed to be handed down, and nobody seemed to know who had them. By this time, Stephanie needed to go to her appointment with the realtor to look at the house she would possibly buy. We asked if we could come back in an hour to ninety minutes for the tour. We were told to come back after the appointment; by then, they would have keys, and everything would be straightened out.

It was ninety minutes before we got back. Staff had changed over, and the group of people we had been talking to had left. They left us a phone number and said that we would have to do the tour at another time. However, when I called about the tour, the guy on the phone said that there were only certain times they gave tours. We would have to wait. The information we were given before was wrong.

After our trip, I did a lot of calling and research about getting on a tour. At one time, the administration was OK with having people tour the sanatorium. In fact, they had a local paranormal team handle it. I talked to them, and they said you had to book with the museum. Once you are booked, then you can go on the tour with them. But when I called the museum, they said they weren't doing tours anymore because there were people still living in the buildings around the sanatorium. It was a housing project for the mentally disabled. The original sanatorium building remained vacant, but all of the other buildings were still being used. After a while of going around in circles, I gave up.

As of this writing, I have called again to see if I could get information about the museum and the tours. I left a couple of messages on the museum's phone message service, but I have yet to get a call back. I'm not really sure whether you can get a tour or if they have nixed that all together. I'm not even sure they know.

What I do know is that the sanatorium holds the energy of some really dreary history, and you can feel it just by walking around the facility. You don't need to go in to feel it. You can go on the premises, and you can drive around. Just be polite and be aware that there are still people working and living there. They don't like talking about the haunted aspect of the institution's history in person, which I think is weird, since they had information for paranormal tours on their website. And there are tons of videos and articles online about the haunted history of the place.

I guess it's some kind of a sanatorium "fight club" rule. First rule of the giant, looming haunted sanatorium is that we don't talk about it being haunted. Maybe someday I'll get a straight answer. Today is not that day.

PART III

FORGOTTEN FACES

CRESCENT HOTEL

75 PROSPECT AVENUE
EUREKA SPRINGS, ARKANSAS 72632

The Crescent Hotel has a rich and winding history. Most people know of it because of its ghosts. It's touted as one of the most haunted hotels in the United States. I've stayed in the hotel, and I have investigated its hallways. I can assure you that it's haunted. It's a consistent battery for paranormal activity. It doesn't matter what time of day it is; when you walk into the hotel, there's a very good chance you will experience something supernatural.

The Crescent Hotel has a great open policy when it comes to the paranormal. The hotel staff and even the management know that the building is haunted, and they cater to it. You don't have to be a guest in order to investigate or look around. In fact, if you are brave, you can ask the employees about their stories, and they are happy to tell you their tales. Many times, I have run into other investigators and created a makeshift group for the night, jumping between everyone's rooms to investigate.

That being said, this part of the book is not going to be specifically about ghosts, because there are other aspects of the hotel's history that need more attention. There are women from the college years of the hotel who have rich stories. There are victims of the notorious Baker Cancer Hospital years who get overshadowed by Baker himself. Their stories need to be told.

Now, some of these stories may have a personal investigation attached to it because that's primarily how I met these lost souls who wanted their lives to matter. They wanted their stories to be recognized and felt overshadowed

The Crescent Hotel. *Photo by author.*

by the hoopla of haunted rooms and paranormal activity. It's hard not to talk about the Crescent without going into paranormal mode. However, if you are looking for a book with all the official spooky ghost stories and salacious details, this is not it.

There are tons of books out there that will give you the chills and thrills of a good haunted hotel. But this book is about the forgotten faces and old souls who need remembering. These two approaches may seem identical, but they're different. This book comes from a different place. It's about real lives, people who had real struggles and who suffered at the expense of others. Let's get into it.

A Brief History of the Crescent Hotel

The Crescent Hotel opened its doors in 1886 after two years of construction. It was considered a masterpiece of architecture and opulence. With its stunning views and lavish accommodations, the hotel became the premiere destination for the wealthy.

After fifteen years of service, the Crescent began to dwindle. In 1902, the building was leased to the Frisco Railroad for five years. Then it became the

Crescent College, which housed women and gave them an opportunity for education and growth. The college soon had a reputation for its commitment to excellence and empowering women. Women came from all over the country to study there.

In 1925, Claude Fuller, U.S. congressman for Arkansas's Third District, and Albert G. Ingals, the mayor of Eureka Springs, bought the hotel. In 1934, the women's college closed its doors. The building remained dormant for another three years.

In 1937, the unscrupulous Norman Baker bought the Crescent and turned it into the Baker Cancer Clinic. He claimed to have created a "cure" for cancer without any kind of surgical procedures. His preposterous proclamations were aired over his radio station and even attracted the attention of the American Medical Association.

Baker renovated the hotel, painting it a lavender hue since his favorite color was purple. He created a secret staircase that went to his office suite and put a morgue in the basement. His unethical medical practices and a slew of dying patients proved that he was a fake and a fraud. However, he was not tried or convicted for what he did at the cancer clinic. In 1940, he was imprisoned for mail fraud.

After Baker's downfall, the Crescent Hotel remained dormant for six years. In 1946, the hotel changed hands. A group of four investors took over the hotel with the vision of renovating it to its former glory. They partnered with the Frisco Railroad to create all-inclusive travel packages, which included scenic train journeys and a luxurious stay at the hotel with all the amenities. This strategy made the Crescent a premier destination again.

In 1967, faulty wiring started a fire that burned the hotel's penthouse and portions of the fourth floor. Necessary renovations and repairs were implemented. Between 1970 and 1972, the hotel changed hands twice. Crescent Heights Development Inc. bought the building and decided the hotel needed a modern upgrade. In a phased approach, it started renovations to bring in new contemporary amenities and give the building a facelift. During this time, the first accounts of paranormal activity were mentioned.

In 1980, the Riverview Management of Arkansas Inc. became a partner investor. In 1985, Willie Nelson played a sold-out show in the Crystal Banquet Room, and then-Governor Bill Clinton gave a keynote speech at the annual chamber banquet. In 1988, the building was acquired by the Wichita Federal Savings and Loan of Wichita and then sold to Gary and Carole Clawson.

By the 1990s, the Crescent was in disrepair and nearly ruined. In 1997, Marty and Elise Roenigk bought the dilapidated building and started renovations. In 2000, the couple had a garden party outside the premises and announced their ten-year plan to fully renovate the hotel. The plan took only five years.

For part of the renovations, they fixed the fifth-floor penthouses that had been devastated by the 1967 fire. They redesigned the sizes of the bedrooms and furnished them with historically accurate furniture. A conservatory was built on the foundation of the old Crescent College Conservatory. Weddings were offered here, and the basement was renovated to incorporate a spa.

In 2009, Marty Roenigk died tragically in a car accident. His wife, Ellie, continues to keep his vision and legacy alive.

PARANORMAL PARASITES: THOUGHTFORMS AND EGREGORES

In the Witch Tok community, there is a lot of talk about egregores. A witch posted a video about how she believes that Trump has an egregore that keeps him from being properly hexed. The video went viral, and there seems to be a lot of interest in the mechanics of an egregore and, more specifically, how one is created. People are speculating about how they're formed and how they exist, making them much more polarized than they need to be.

Egregores are common occurrences. They are an accumulation of thoughts and emotions that take on a collective consciousness. Most churches or places of worship have an egregore. Have you ever walked into a church and felt the energy of reverence? That's the collective consciousness of all the prayers, sermons and rituals that have been performed there. That's an egregore.

Thought forms have a similar structure. They are more focused, as they are usually the concoction of just one or two people. They can be programmed with the intention of a singular purpose. Or they can start off as a seed of an idea and then morph into an egregore when more people put energy into them. Both thoughtforms and egregores require consistent energy. The more energy you put into it, the stronger it gets. The energy can be shifted and changed, but it will always require a feeding source.

The Philip experiment is the most popular example of a thoughtform experiment. The Philip experiment, conducted in 1972 by the Toronto Parapsychological Research Society, was overseen by Dr. A.R. George Owen.

It involved a group of ten individuals who employed a methodical approach to invent a fictional ghost named Philip Aylesford and then endeavored to communicate with this entity through a séance. The character's life story was crafted with a blend of real and fabricated events, intentionally incorporating timeline discrepancies and clear contradictions to observe their real-world manifestations.

Philip Ayelsford's backstory begins with his birth in 1624 in England. Enlisting in the military as a youth, he was knighted at the age of sixteen. Throughout his military tenure, he served as a spy for Charles II and took part in the English Civil War. It was during his service to the king that Philip encountered Dorothea, a nobleman's daughter. Struck by her sweetness and beauty, he eventually married her.

Following their marriage, Dorothea became distant and unpleasant toward Philip. Her volatile temper surfaced, and she frequently initiated quarrels with him. Disenchanted with the marriage, Philip sought comfort elsewhere. He prolonged his absences by riding through the forest to avoid returning home.

On one such ride, he encountered a group of itinerant Romani people. His attention was captured by a woman named Margo, who possessed striking blue eyes. They were instantly smitten with each other, unwilling to part. Philip brought Margo back to his family's estate, concealing her presence while he contemplated the future of his marriage and what to do about his wife.

Dorothea, suspecting foul play, discovered the Romani woman's secret refuge. In a fit of rage and seeking vengeance, she falsely charged Margo with witchcraft, leading to her arrest. Paralyzed by fear and uncertainty, Philip remained silent throughout Margo's trial and could only watch in silence as she was executed by fire. Devastated by the ordeal, Philip took his own life, passing away at the age of thirty.

Subsequently, a group formed with the intent to contact Philip's spirit. They convened weekly, encircling a table to meditate in unison. The stipulation was that the participants had to maintain a jovial spirit and harbor an unwavering conviction in Philip's eventual manifestation. This practice continued for an entire year, yet it yielded no tangible proof of contact with Philip.

In their frustration, the group opted to switch their meeting approach to traditional nineteenth-century séance and table-tipping methods. Four sessions later, they experienced success. When a member summoned Philip, the table vibrated and produced a clear knock.

The team established a knocking system: one knock for "yes" and two for "no." They queried the backstory of their fictional character, Philip, to which he responded with complete accuracy. As belief in Philip grew, so did the paranormal occurrences; he soon demonstrated the ability to tip tables, levitate items and disrupt lighting. Over four years, the group engaged with Philip, holding televised table-tipping sessions and numerous interviews. Despite the experiment's apparent success, Owens deemed it unsuccessful because the group had failed to manifest Philip as a full-bodied ghost. While various theories exist, the prevailing belief is that the phenomena observed during the Philip experiment can be attributed to psychokinesis.

In 2007, I created my own thoughtform experiment with a group of investigators in a haunted hotel, using the Philip experiment as a model. In the Pearl experiment, participants utilized the Glen Tavern Inn's richly haunted past to fabricate a backstory for a nonexistent ghost, detailing manifestations for credibility. They aimed to circulate this invented ghost tale among other paranormal investigators to observe if any haunting evidence would emerge. The creation process unfolded as follows:

The entity was designated female early in the process, contrasting the male "Philip" from the Philip experiment. The first floor of the Glen Tavern Inn was home to vibrant female specters whose narratives could be adapted for the new thoughtform ghost. The group saw this as an advantageous setting. They wove the thoughtform's backstory into the inn's existing lore, enhancing its authenticity by aligning her story with preexisting ghostly tales.

Collectively, the participants envisioned her appearance, attire and life story, opting for a macabre demise to intensify interest and potentially aid in eliciting electronic voice phenomena, including distinctive sounds, like the clinking of coins.

The entire group concurred on discussing the newly conceived ghostly entity. The plan was to incorporate her into articles and disseminate her spectral tales as though she had always been woven into the history of the Glen Tavern Inn. The aim was to lend credibility to her narrative, spark interest in her investigation and perhaps gather proof to substantiate her existence.

During the third week of July 2007, the activation ritual was performed in the lobby of the Glen Tavern Inn in the middle of the night. The ceremony began with a circle and the invocation of the four corners. Each participant in the circle read Pearl's description aloud. Additional invocations were recited to anchor her into reality and manifest her existence. A candle was then lit, and subsequently, the circle was closed.

Following the ceremony, the members of the group dispersed to attend the conference and resumed their individual activities. Discussions about Pearl subsided for several months. Although the creation of Pearl was not forgotten, the group agreed that the thoughtform required time to gather energy and reveal herself.

In November 2008, a member of the original ritual was contacted by a couple who had visited the Glen Tavern Inn and captured an image of a woman in a green dress bearing a striking resemblance to Pearl. This couple was unaware of the paranormal convention and had no connections with any of the circle's founding members.

The photograph was captured in a corridor between two mirror-lined rooms. Reflected in the mirror is the side profile of a woman with dark brown hair wearing a green dress and looking toward the photographer. At the moment the photo was taken, there were no other women in or near the room, according to the couple. They believed they were alone, given the late hour of their investigation. They also recalled that no one else at the hotel matched the description of the woman in the photograph. Upon seeing the photo, the original group member immediately recognized the entity as Pearl, the thoughtform.

Essentially, our thoughtform had manifested itself as a ghost. It's now one of the apparitions paranormal investigators see at the hotel. Her story has changed, and it's become attached to two other female ghosts on the first floor. Pearl's story is interchangeable with theirs, which feeds into the energy as a whole.

But even though our thoughtform never existed as a real person, her ghost is tangible and can communicate. I've done full-on spirit communication sessions with her. She creates EVPs. She has manipulated lights and interacted with physical equipment. Other investigators who don't know she is a manufactured ghost have interacted with Pearl. They have gotten tangible results. She presents as an intelligent haunting.

Thoughtforms and Egregores at the Crescent Hotel

Most of the popular ghosts that are highly publicized at the Crescent are probably thoughtforms or egregores. This is a common phenomenon that nobody talks about because it takes away the audacious spooky factor of a haunted hotel. We want to believe ghosts are real because it proves that there is some kind of afterlife. That our energy lingers and at least does something after our death, even if it just tours the same halls of the same hotel for eternity. At least that's better than ceasing to exist. We all want to be remembered. However, the reality is that most of the ghosts at the Crescent were never real people. They never existed. They are stories that have turned into folklore and been sensationalized through consistent retellings.

Every haunted hotel has a lady in white. There are always children playing down the halls of the second floor. A mischievous ghost, usually a man, always likes to mess with the ladies. There is always a woman who messes with the room or with the luggage or tidies things up. And there is always a pregnant woman who jumps out a window or dies by suicide because her love doesn't want anything to do with the situation (usually because he is married or because the situation is a secret).

The following is a list of the most prominent ghosts in the Crescent Hotel. I got this list from the book *The Crescent Hotel*, by Susan Schafer. It's the one they sell in the lobby gift shop. The shop's centerpiece is Norman Baker's gigantic wooden desk. It's a beautiful piece, and most people don't realize they are looking at a piece of macabre history. You can buy cards in a set. Each has the sketch of a ghost and a description of them on the back. The sketches are the same ones found in the book, and the descriptions are very similar. The following list provides a brief synopsis of each ghost.

- Michael: He resides in Room 218. He's good-looking, mischievous and likes to "flirt" with women.
- The Young Boy (Breckie): He's a four-year-old with blond hair, blue eyes and a ball who can usually be seen on the second or third floor.
- The Little Girl: She fell to her death through the spindles on the fourth floor of the main staircase. She stays up on the top floor.
- The Lady in White (The Nurse): She's in her late thirties or early forties, and she wheels a gurney on the third floor.
- The College Girl: She was a young woman from the women's college who fell out of a window on the third floor. There were rumors she had an affair with an older man.
- Theodora: She resides in room 419. She was a housekeeper or a nurse. She likes to tidy up rooms and pack people's bags.

This is not a coincidence. If you go to any haunted hotel—it doesn't matter the location—you will have a similar set of ghosts. The stories and personalities will be different. They will usually coincide with the history of property, but they will generally have the same tropes and similar backstories.

The Crescent Hotel has an unusual aspect to its history, because it was a wellness hospital for a while. So, nurses are walking down the hallways along with the ghostly children. It makes for a creepier atmosphere, and it brings in the curious and the morbid. There are daily ghost tours. The same stories are told over and over. There have been seventeen TV shows filmed in the location, talking about the same ghosts and looking for the same kind of paranormal phenomenon.

All that energy creates an expectation of how the paranormal will respond. How the activity will present itself. The paranormal energy is constantly being fed and curated. Eventually, all that energy has to do something. It collects and curates an egregore that acts like a ghost. It will interact with you. It will create knocks. It will manipulate EMF detectors. It will adhere to the story that has been told over and over and over.

If a new element is added—as long as it's talked about—the egregore will adapt. For example, if a white woman is seen walking up the stairs, someone may mention that she smells like French perfume. Then other people will start talking about how the white lady who walks up the stairs smells like perfume. It could be French perfume, or maybe it's lavender. After a while, this detail will become part of the mythology, and the smell of French lavender perfume will be smelled by anyone who walks up the stairway. Thoughtforms and egregores literally adapt and mimic the energy that is being fed to them.

Once you realize this, paranormal activity becomes very routine. The similarities become obvious, and it's easier to parse out the thought forms from the real activity. Aside from the typical ghost tropes, there are real lives, real people who want to come through. They want to communicate their stories. They want to be remembered. Sometimes, it's hard to know the difference.

I've encountered most of the typical paranormal activity at the Crescent Hotel. I've had experiences with all of the ghosts on the tour, almost like it was too easy. But then I tend to recognize egregore energy and can feed into its desire to mimic. I believe that most of the activity in the Crescent Hotel is part of this phenomenon.

NORMAN BAKER

I didn't want to write this section because there is too much written about this conman and his crimes. He's been sensationalized due to his audacity, but really, he just ruined people's lives. In my mind, he is a murderer and thief. He is one of the grossest dregs of humanity. That being said, he plays such a large role in the narrative of the Crescent Hotel, it's hard not to talk about those who suffered and were ultimately forgotten there without bringing him into the fold.

Baker gave false hope. He brought people to his wellness center with the promise of a better life, only to strip it away and dump their bodies in the dark of night. He wrote letters to their loved ones, pretending they were getting better. He asked for more money. He alluded there was more time, knowing full well there was none. Baker sucked the life out of his victims, and now, his portrait hangs on the wall of the Crescent in full display. I'll give the run-down here for context. However, he is in no way the focus. He is just a depraved man with blood on his hands.

Norman Baker was born on November 27, 1882. He was the youngest of ten children. At sixteen, he became a machinist. Then he worked as a die

Norman Baker. *Photo by author.*

and toolmaker. He would travel from town to town looking for work. After watching a mentalist named "Professor Flint," Baker was inspired to create his own show.

He hit the road with his act, using the name "Charles Welsh," and he employed a woman whom he named "Madame Pearl Tangely" to be his female counterpart. When she quit in 1909, Baker employed Theresa Pinder to replace her, and she even used the same name. Pinder would eventually become his wife. The show ran successfully for another five years.

In 1915, Baker invented a calliope that used air instead of steam. He called it the air calliaphone and sold three of them in a short period. He decided to quit the vaudeville circuit and started a manufacturing business for his new invention. In 1916, he divorced his wife and focused his energy on his new venture.

His business quickly became a success, and in the first year, he made over $60,000 in sales. Baker boasted that at the height of his business, he had made over $200,000 in sales in a year. Altogether, the calliope manufacturing business made over $1.5 million in sales.

In 1920, the manufacturing factory of Baker's business burned down. He created a correspondence art school and mail-order business to fund the rebuilding of the factory. The art school ran for three years, but once the calliope manufacturing proved to be profitable again, he closed it down.

In 1925, Baker requested the Muscatine Chamber of Commerce to sponsor his idea for a radio station. He would call it *Know the Naked Truth* (*KTNT*) and focus on local politics. On Thanksgiving that same year, he aired his first show. Baker was licensed for only five hundred watts, but he routinely aired at around ten thousand watts to reach the largest amount of people possible. In 1928, Baker was officially licensed to air at ten thousand watts, and his radio show reached around one million homes.

He used his new media platform to broadcast local news intertwined with anti-Jewish, pro-Hitler propaganda, which he used to attack the American Medical Association.

According to the book *Quacks and Crusaders*, Baker would allude to the idea that all doctors were pedophiles.

> *Baker also invoked horrific images of physicians as pedophiles, asking KTNT listeners why doctors vaccinated young children in the leg rather than in the arm. "Is it because they like to feel the legs of these innocent little girls?" he asked. "Is it not a fact that many of these men use their profession as an excuse to fondle and gaze upon the nude parts of innocent children."*

Baker created a fever pitch of fear around doctors with his rhetoric and then leveraged it by touting his own cures for cancer. The American Medical Association lobbied the Federal Trade Commission to have Baker taken off the air. On June 5, 1931, KTNT was officially taken off the air.

The businessman persisted, and in 1933, he took his radio show to Mexico and changed its name. The new show was called *XENT*, and he was licensed the same number of watts. So, he was able to re-create a steady following very quickly without any kind of monitoring.

In 1929, Baker opened the Baker Institute at Muscatine. On his radio station and in its accompanying magazine, the businessman claimed to have the cure for cancer. He said he got it from Dr. Ozias, who had his own cancer institute in Kansas City. Ozias claimed he had gotten the cure from a secret witch doctor. The "cure" was given by injection and made of all-natural ingredients.

In an article in Baker's magazine, he offered to give five patients the amazing cure for free to prove its effectiveness. One by one, each "lucky" patient died, but Baker lied in his magazine and on his radio show, touting everyone's health had improved.

People believed his rhetoric and truly believed that Baker had the magical cure. In its first year of business, the Baker Institute made around $444,000 in earnings. The American Medical Association believed Baker was a fraud and did everything it could to get him closed down. The *Journal of the American Medical Association* wrote in its April edition, "The viciousness of Mr. Baker's broadcasting lies not in what he says about the American Medical Association but in the fact that he induces sufferers from cancer who might have some chance for their lives, if seen early and properly treated, to resort to his nostrum."

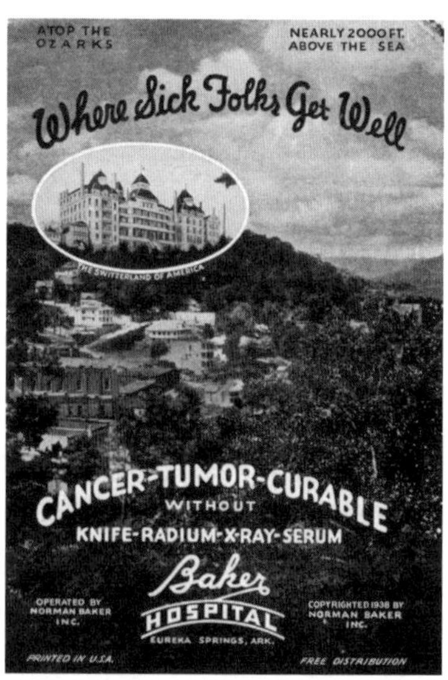

Cancer Cure Center pamphlet. *Photo by author.*

Eventually, the association was able to get a warrant for Baker's arrest, as he was practicing medicine without a license. This was around the same time the businessman had his radio station closed. So, Baker went to Mexico to create another radio station and another cancer treatment center.

In 1937, he returned to Muscatine, Iowa, where he spent one day in jail to clear his warrant. Later, he ran for governor of Iowa and then for the Iowa State Senate. Both times, he lost. So, he regrouped and decided to move to Arkansas, where he leased the Crescent Hotel.

During this time, the hotel was in disrepair. At first, the Eureka Springs Chamber of Commerce was excited for Baker to rejuvenate the area. They believed that the new cancer center would bring more tourism to the city.

Baker renovated the Crescent Hotel by painting the penthouse, office and lobby, with its giant fireplace, purple. He hung guns on the walls and created secret passageways throughout the hotel, just in case he had to leave quickly. He also added a morgue in the basement.

The cancer center brought in a lot of people, and in his first year, Baker made over $500,000. Just like he had at his other cancer centers, Baker never created a true cure, and his patients kept dying. The businessman ran the center for two years and then was arrested for mail fraud. He served four years in prison.

In the senior associate's warden report, Baker stated as an inmate:

> *I am not guilty. They have never proved anything in the indictment. We figure this was a railroading proposition. It is my opinion that the jury was fixed and influenced. We have hired private detectives to look into the matter. It is believed that whiskey and women were made available to the jurors. We were railroaded by the American Medical Association who have been after us for years.*

Baker was released in 1944 and moved to Florida to retire. In 1958, Baker died of cirrhosis of the liver.

WHAT'S IN THE JARS?

On February 5, 2019, a landscaper found a dump site of bottles and jars while using a backhoe to renovate the land and make way for an archery range. After the police and other officials checked the site, it was theorized that the artifacts were a part of the hotel's Norman Baker Cancer Cure Center era.

In the cachet, twenty of the bottles contained what seemed to be human tissue preserved in alcohol. Over one hundred other jars may have

The jars wall display in the Crescent Hotel. *Photo by author.*

contained other specimens of human tissue, but the lids were unscrewed, which let the alcohol escape and the contents decay. Some of the bottles contained Norman Baker's cancer concoction, called "Cure #5," which was made of ground watermelon seed, red clover, corn silk, peppermint, glycerin and carbolic acid. Sometimes, it had water or alcohol in it to be used as a preservative.

According to the local lore, Baker decorated the morgue with jars full of tumors he had removed from his patients. The hospital's magazine ran an advertisement with pictures of the bottles and the caption, "We have hundreds of specimens like these....Actual cancer specimens and laboratory data proves all....All specimens are preserved in alcohol."

It is believed that Baker probably bought the specimens and brought them into the Crescent Hotel. Or maybe they were part of his other cancer institute in Iowa that was closed because Baker had a warrant for practicing medicine without a license. During the twenty months the hotel was a cancer center, forty bodies ended up in the morgue. Allegedly, none of them were operated on because Baker had no surgical training. He was a con man and radio personality. He wasn't someone to get his hands dirty—literally.

According to a YouTube video called "Bottles from 1886 Crescent Hotel EXPOSED!" by Larry Flaxman, the University of Arkansas was supposed to test some of the jar specimens to see if they contained human tissue. After three years, nothing happened. So, Flaxman asked for permission from the hotel to take a specimen to have it privately analyzed.

The jars in the basement. *Photo by author.*

The following is an excerpt of his account in the YouTube video:

> *Because of the historical significance, the University of Arkansas was called in to conduct a full archeological survey, and they took numerous bottles and containers back to their lab for analysis. Three years later, the university, unfortunately, still had not provided any information about the samples, and we were becoming increasingly frustrated by the lack of communication or resolution. During the 2022 ESP weekend in January, I offered to help.*
>
> *Hotel management quickly agreed, and I took several bottles, including one containing potential human tissue, back home for analysis. I spent the next six months looking for a pathology lab that could perform the forensic analysis on these eighty-plus-year-old samples.*
>
> *The project turned out to be far more difficult than I had anticipated. I was encountering roadblocks at every turn. After exhausting nearly all of my options, I finally received a positive response.*
>
> *That long-awaited email came from surgical pathologist Dr. Charles M. Quick, who was intrigued enough by the project to agree to meet with me and see if these samples were viable or had degraded too much due to the passage of time or their unfavorable storage conditions.*

Dr. Charles M. Quick is an academic surgical pathologist who specializes in women's oncology. He has been in the field since 2005, and his job is to look at tissue to see if it's diseased. In the video, he said that he didn't know about the jars at the Crescent Hotel but was intrigued. He agreed to look at the contents of the jar.

He said he was skeptical at first, assuming the contents were animal tissue. However, upon looking at the tissue, he realized right away that it was a blood clot. He said it had a rubbery consistency that would be hard to re-create with artificial materials.

The following is what Dr. Quick said in the video:

> *It did look biologic, which was both pleasantly surprising and somewhat shocking at the same time. Relatively well preserved, too. Not sure what was in the bottle, but whatever it was, the way that it was preserved actually kept it pretty well. And yeah, seeing that initially was surprising…*
>
> *You feel the rubbery consistency,* [which] *kind of tells you, oh, this could be clotted blood as opposed to something that will be hard, like bone, or tough and rubbery, like muscle. And after a while, you get used to feeling these different textures, and then we cut the tissue up and look at it, and what you're looking for is anything that stands out.*
>
> *Little tan spots, white flecks. Any differences in color, consistency, texture. And then anytime you see that difference, you would want to take little pieces of it, which is what we did,* [from] *several of the different areas from across the tissue specimen. We submit that in, and we process it using some different chemicals, which fixes it, further firms it up, if you will….*
>
> *We take the tissue, they embed it in wax, and then we cut that tissue, about the thickness of human hair or half a human hair—towards basically transparent—put it on a glass slide and stain it with chemicals… which turn certain things pink, certain things purple, certain things shades of blue, et cetera.*

During Dr. Quick's analysis, he said that he had some unexpected findings, and the blood clot had bonus material. Once he started looking at it under the microscope, he realized it had fibrous connective tissue, stroma and muscle.

Dr. Quick realized the specimen had been taken out of the patient during a surgery. This confused him because, according to Baker, there were never any surgeries conducted at the Crescent Hotel. The big draw was that his miracle cure negated surgery all together.

Dr. Quick said the tissue was not cancerous, but it was diseased tissue. It was infected. He also found fibrous cotton material on the specimen, which is used in Q-tips and cotton gauze.

The following is what Dr. Quick said in his own words:

> *Cotton gauze, which, I mean, has been around for ages. And you use cotton gauze to—to pack wounds.…You wouldn't always just cut this off immediately, right? You pack it with cotton gauze, usually soaked in some kind of antiseptic material. And that would theoretically maybe stop bacteria from growing in the wound and maybe help it to heal.*
>
> *It doesn't always work, especially if the wound is bad. Then you progress to surgery. So, what do you do? You pack the wound with gauze. When we found evidence of gauze within the wound…we still, to this day…what we'd call a secondary intention wound, which is a wound that we don't suture together, right?*
>
> *So, a wound that you leave open that then heals slowly over time, right? So, one of these wounds, we would still to this day take medicated gauze. We would pack it, we'd change it on a regular basis, irrigate the wound, keep things clean, and help it to heal on its own while preventing infection. And this is very similar to what was happening even when this theoretical patient was being treated.*

Dr. Quick said he also found vegetable material in the specimen. Flaxman asked what that meant. Dr. Quick revealed that it was poop. He stated that patients with illness are not able to go to the bathroom because they are bedridden. Also, they are not able to bathe. A nurse would have had to bathe the theoretical patient and wouldn't have been able to do a perfect job. Dr. Quick said, to this day, nurses have a hard time keeping patients completely clean.

The following is his assessment of what happened:

> *If you can imagine, someone very sick with cancer being treated would be bedridden. So, this is just basic care. This is basic care, right? This is something that happens to patients that are in the hospital for long periods of time that you have to treat, because if you don't, they could get septic and die.*
>
> *And this is outside of the realm of cancer care per se. But it is part of what you would do to take care of a patient that had been inpatient in a hospital, in a bed for a long period of time.…Pressure sores can set in pretty quickly, especially if the patient's not moved around very often.*

> *Putting all of it together, knowing the location, knowing the time period, knowing what was happening at this location I think it's very reasonable to say that you're looking at tissue from a patient that was inpatient at that hospital, tissue that had to be removed because it became an infected wound.*
>
> *And so, they cut it and kept it. Why they kept it in the manner they kept it, I don't know. I'm glad they did, because if they wouldn't have, then we would've never seen it. But what it does show is that there were people there that had common complications to being an inpatient in a hospital setting, and that they were being treated.*

Dr. Quick went on to say that it's proof the center had some kind of clinical care. If Baker kept this tissue, then it was part of some kind of showmanship. To show new patients that they would be well taken care of during their stay.

If you want more information about the Crescent Hotel or the jars, check out Larry's website: www.larryflaxman.com.

Did the jars come from the patients in the Crescent? Was Baker keeping the bed sores of his patients as some kind of showmanship? To prove that he had the best cancer facility? Or did he buy them in Iowa and bring them for the sheer showmanship of it all?

We will never know. However, a part of someone's body is forever trapped in a time capsule of preserving liquid. It's unfortunate we don't know that person's story and what they went through. It might put some humanity back into the jars instead and make them something more than a set of macabre props in the hotel's basement.

THE GIRL IN THE BASEMENT

I have seen the jars up close and personal. There's a room in the Crescent Hotel's basement that used to be the old morgue. Why do you need a morgue with a giant freezer in at a cancer cure center? I don't know. That's a question for Mr. Baker.

Here's the official version of the story from the Ozarks Alive website:

> *It was once used as the kitchen, but later became the morgue and its walk-in cooler a place to store the bodies of deceased patients. Most folks who were near death were sent home to die…but ones who didn't make it there came to the morgue after being sequestered to what became known as the asylum.*

You can only get down into the basement if you pay for the ghost tour. So, of course I did just that. My mom went with me, and we spent a good amount of time picking up those jars and staring at them. They give off weird feelings. There's something unnatural about them. It's a combination of sadness, uncertainty and claustrophobia. I'm not sure how else to describe it. When I touched it, I felt a sense of the earth closing in around me. It made me want to get out of the room and leave the basement. I felt very uneasy and unsettled. I felt trapped.

Another time, I was investigating the hallway that goes to the basement with a group of investigators. I came with a handful of investigators, and as we investigated the hallways of the hotel, we kept collecting people. By the end of the night, as we got to the lowest part of the building, we had over ten people with us.

We went to the halfway point of the hallway and sat down. There was a very strange feeling in this area, and we felt this would be the best place to do an impromptu spirit communication session. Everyone got settled and quieted down. We sat in silence while one of the women in our group started a session. The activity picked up pretty quickly.

There seems to be a low-level energy that likes to show itself in that area. I've experienced it a few times, and it doesn't surprise me, even though others were freaking out and pronouncing it a demon. It's not. According to the Crescent Hotel's website, "A dark figure has been seen recently in the morgue and there has been an increase in cold spots and reports of people being touched."

I'm pretty sure this is what we were experiencing. It's more like a thought orm. It doesn't have enough intelligence to be anything more. That's why it shows up as a dark figure.

There was a curious incident that did stick with me, though. There was a young girl that came through. She said she wanted her story told. We asked her where she came from and why she was lurking around the basement area. She said that pieces of her were being kept in one of the jars. So, she remains down there because she feels attached to the place. During the communication session, we asked if she died in the building, and she said no. I thought it was a little eerie that she would want to stay with the physical pieces of her body. Why not stay with the rest of her body?

I didn't take the communication very seriously that night. There were a lot of people, and it was late in the evening. Everyone was tired, and I wasn't sure if what we gotten had any merit. This wasn't my usual investigation team, and many of the people in the group were new to investigating and were following our group around because we had equipment and experience.

Later in the week, I kept going back to that communication sequence. There was something about it that didn't sit well with me. Maybe it's because I had touched those jars before. Maybe I felt a lot of empathy for the people who were connected to those jars. Their tissue is just sitting there in liquid, with no respect for their lives. Maybe I was being overly dramatic about it. Maybe I had overlaid my own uneasy experience onto the spirit communication session. These were all good explanations. Even as a psychic, I do tend to try and analyze my own experiences.

As I was writing this book and looking over all of my research about the Crescent Hotel, I did find an article that mentioned a specter of a young girl in the basement. It made me wonder if this was the same spirit we had encountered. I have scoured the internet, but there isn't a lot of information about this spirit. It's not part of the usual lexicon. This is unfortunate because I don't have a lot to go on except my own experience. If she is real, I hope someday she finds some peace and can escape whatever atrocities were done to her.

Who Is Theodora?

Theodora is the "ghost" that I have had the most interactions with, even though I sometimes don't realize I've encountered the ghost until later. Anytime I visit the Crescent Hotel, I tend to gravitate to the fourth floor and sit in front of room 419. It seems to be the quietest of the hotel's floors, even though there's a lot of activity up there. Strangely, the fourth floor houses the ghost tour office and the pizza café. It's also where, on certain nights, a lady specter can be seen jumping off the balcony into the darkened night. I can't remember the exact time she's seen, but I know it's near midnight and I have made sure to be on the grass to witness it. Yet it has not happened on my watch.

All that being said, the fourth floor feels the most relaxed to me, and it's where I like to go to set up my equipment. Many times, I have had full conversations with Theodora using my spirit box. At least I think it's her. It feels like her. The messages I get usually have some kind of strange coincidence attached to them. It's never an immediate cause and effect. It always takes some time to come about, and it always has to do with lost souls or the forgotten.

Maybe I have a special affinity for her because she is said to be the spirit that helps stranded entities find their way home. She seems to be a maternal figure who has a purpose. She feels protective and kind, but she's also a powerhouse. If she doesn't like you, she will make herself known. She seems to represent an archetypal energy: the mother. And sometimes, the guardian.

About four years ago, I went to the Crescent Hotel with an investigation group. We rented out room 419, or Theodora's suite. Within a couple of hours in her suite, our paranormal group had an experience with her. It wasn't the usual experience, with her packing up our stuff or tidying up our room. However, she did repeatedly open the door of the TV stand. I don't know why. We kept closing it, but when we came back later, it was always open. It's a heavy piece of wood. It's not the kind of piece where the door slides open. You have to close it hard to get it to click. I played with it to make sure this wasn't just gravity doing its job.

That was a minor phenomenon. A tedious thing just to show us she was there. What happened next was a different kind of phenomenon. There are two doors in room 419. One is the original door, which leads to the hallway, and it's permanently closed. You can't go in or out. It's there more for decoration, to show how the room was laid out prior to renovations. The second door is around the corner, and that's the one you use to get out of the room.

Our group was sitting in the room, looking around. It was still early in the evening. I don't even think it was dark outside yet. Someone (or something) was outside the original hallway door. We heard some shuffling around, but we didn't hear the jingle of keys like people describe. Then someone knocked loudly on the door. One of our members mentioned something about someone using the wrong door and went to the second door to see who was in the hallway. There was loud banging again. The door was open, and there was no one in the hallway.

You can hear every little sound in that hallway. How do I know? Because every time the ghost tour went by, we could hear the footsteps of everyone settling in the hallway. We had other people go to our front door looking for us, and you could hear their movement. The hotel is not good for privacy if you want to be stealthy. However, we did not hear or see who pounding on the door. And we didn't hear anyone leave.

The air was wrong, too. I don't know how to explain it, but it was too quiet. Too still. It was almost like we were in a vacuum for a few seconds while the phenomenon was happening. It's funny, too. We all agreed that it was Theodora trying to get into her room right away. There was no questioning it. We knew it was her.

I didn't make sense to me why someone like Theodora would want to make herself known to a bunch of paranormal investigators. But a lot of us in that room were psychic. And we don't usually just investigate for the fun of it. I will write about my experiences and make sure they aren't forgotten. Stephanie can channel big energy. She has nurturing empathy. The others in our group were more concerned with the well-being of the entities around us than getting the best evidence.

If Theodora is an entity who looks over all of the other castaway spirits in a liminal space like the Crescent Hotel, then it would make sense that she would want our attention. We would be the kind of people who would pay attention to her and take her seriously. Also, we would listen to her and act on it rather than question it.

But then that begs the question: Who was Theodora?

It depends on who you ask.

Some will tell you she was a patient during the Norman Baker hospital years, lured to the Crescent by promises of miracle cures and then left to die in a building with no medical licensing and no actual doctors. Others claim she was a nurse—possibly one of the few people with real medical knowledge who tried to do what she could for the suffering patients caught in Baker's scam. Some guides say she was both: a caregiver who eventually succumbed to illness herself and died within those walls.

And then there are the others who say Theodora is more than just one woman. She's a construct of many women's energies: patients, nurses, caretakers and maybe even a housekeeper or two. Ghosts who, in death, merged into one spectral personality. The neat freak with a purpose. The maternal guide. The opinionated protector. The one who helps the others cross over. Again, an archetype.

Her origin is as fractured as the fourth-floor renovation, which left room 419 with two doors and a hallway no one uses. There's no official record of a "Theodora" at Baker's hospital. No obituary, no census trail, no medical chart. But that's true for many who passed through that place. Baker wasn't known for his bookkeeping. And the ones who died there didn't exactly get sent off with dignity.

What we do have are the stories.

The most common version goes like this: Theodora is a polite, older woman dressed in 1930s fashion. She's often seen outside room 419, rummaging through her purse for her keys. She'll smile, nod, maybe say hello. And then she'll vanish. Housekeepers have reported her introducing herself by name, even going so far as to explain that she's "Dr. Baker's patient." That's where the story and the name originated. One chance encounter with a spirit who identified herself, and decades of ghost lore were born.

She's not one of those ghosts who lurks in the shadows or sends people running down the hallway. She doesn't need to. Her presence is felt through small, deliberate actions. She opens drawers. She tucks people in. She folds your clothes and reorganizes your space when you're being disrespectful or chaotic. She communicates through tidiness. Through structure. Through the kind of psychic language only people tuned into the subtle can really decode.

Multiple guests have shared eerily similar stories: finding jewelry lined up in neat rows, bags packed and zipped by the door after a fight, shoes arranged where they weren't before. She's not malicious. But she has boundaries. If she doesn't like the energy you bring into her room, she'll show you the door—sometimes literally.

And it's that intentionality that makes her stand out.

She doesn't feel trapped. She doesn't feel confused or stuck in a loop like some of the other spirits at the Crescent. She feels present. Aware. Maybe even a little purposeful, like she's chosen to stay not because she can't move on but because someone needs to keep things in order. She's the kind of ghost who seems more interested in the other spirits than the people who bump into her during ghost tours. She has a job, and she's still doing it.

Some psychic mediums say she's a gatekeeper. That she helps souls transition out of the Crescent when they're ready. Others believe she's tied to the room itself, assigned to it in death the same way a nurse might be assigned to a wing in life. A few go further, calling her an energetic "anchor."

And then there are the outlier stories in which Theodora doesn't feel quite so tidy. In those, she's forceful, even disruptive. Knocking on doors. Slamming drawers. Creating pockets of silence that feel unnatural, like reality is momentarily suspended. Like my group experienced that night.

That leads to my theory, which is that Theodora isn't a single spirit at all. She's probably an egregore. There are theories among Crescent historians and ghost tour guides that say Theodora is a composite spirit. Instead of separating the encounters into multiple ghost profiles, they have all been folded into one character. That's not uncommon in haunted places. Paranormal lore tends to congeal around the most popular or most persistent names. Ghosts, like legends, often survive because they've been given a face. A voice. A name.

That doesn't make Theodora any less real. In fact, it might make her more real. Because whatever she is—a single woman with a powerful will or a chorus of echoes speaking through one name—her presence is undeniable. She continues to interact. She continues to communicate. And she continues to matter.

Maybe that's why she reached out to our group. We weren't there for cheap thrills. We weren't trying to provoke or record something to boost our online views. We were listening. Feeling. Asking. And she felt that. Maybe she needed our attention. Maybe she wanted you to know that room 419 isn't just a haunted attraction. It's a space she's still stewarding. A liminal zone where lost souls drift in and out. She stands at the doorway, checking their energy and deciding whether they're ready to leave.

That would explain the knocking. The cold stillness. The feeling of being held in place by something unseen but deliberate. Maybe she was asking you to listen. Or maybe she was just reminding us that, while Norman Baker's crimes may have erased the identities of so many who passed through his fake hospital, someone like Theodora is making sure they're not forgotten.

Theodora's presence in room 419 is undeniable. Her actions suggest a consciousness that transcends a singular identity. Theodora's consistent manifestations mirror the characteristics of a collective egregore that decided to take on an archetypical role. Consider the myriad stories: a woman in 1930s attire searching for her keys, the meticulous organization of personal items, the protective aura felt by many. These accounts, while varied, share a common thread a maternal presence. This consistency suggests not just a singular spirit but a collective embodiment of the hotel's history and the emotions of those who have passed through its halls.

Theodora's interactions aren't limited to passive observations. She engages, responds and even corrects, as seen in instances where guests have found their belongings rearranged or received unexpected knocks on the door. Such behaviors align with the concept of an egregore influencing its environment and those within it.

Moreover, the energy surrounding room 419 is palpable. Visitors often describe a distinct atmosphere—a blend of warmth, vigilance and an unspoken expectation of respect. This ambiance, cultivated over decades, reinforces the idea of a collective consciousness at play.

In this light, Theodora transcends the traditional definition of a ghost. She embodies the memories, emotions and energies of countless individuals connected to the Crescent Hotel. As an egregore, she serves as both guardian and guide, ensuring that the stories of the past remain alive and that the space she inhabits is treated with the reverence it deserves.

Theodora as Guardian of the Liminal

Theodora's presence in room 419 transcends the typical ghost story. Whether she was once a patient, a nurse or a housekeeper, her essence has evolved into something more profound. She's a protector, a guide and, perhaps, an egregore formed by collective memory and emotion.

In contrast, the lingering energy of Norman Baker permeates the lower levels of the Crescent Hotel. His presence isn't necessarily his spirit; instead, it's an egregore fueled by the continuous retelling of his dark history, his desk prominently displayed in the lounge and the artifacts unearthed from his time. This energy is palpable, especially in the basement and on the first floor, where guests often report feelings of unease. Interestingly, room 419 sits directly beneath what was once Norman Baker's penthouse.

Despite their proximity, the energies between the two spaces couldn't be more contrasting. The lower floors, especially the basement, often exude a heavy, oppressive atmosphere—an egregore of Baker's dark legacy, fueled by continuous retellings and the artifacts displayed throughout the hotel. In contrast, the fourth floor, under Theodora's watch, feels subdued and calm. It's as if she acts as a barrier, preventing the malevolent energy from ascending.

Yet ascending to the fourth floor brings a noticeable shift. The atmosphere becomes quieter, more subdued. Despite room 419 being located directly beneath Baker's former penthouse, it's as if Theodora's presence acts as a barrier, keeping the oppressive energy at bay. She maintains a sanctuary amid the residual darkness, ensuring that the upper levels remain a place of peace and reflection

Theodora embodies the role of a gatekeeper, overseeing the transition between the living and the departed. Her actions—organizing belongings, comforting guests and asserting boundaries—reflect a deep commitment to maintaining balance within the hotel. She ensures that the stories of those who suffered are remembered with dignity and that the space remains a haven for both spirits and visitors alike.

IN HIS OWN WORDS

I think the most frustrating part of writing about the Crescent Hotel is the lack of focus on the patients of Baker's cancer cure center. He had two. He started his shenanigans in Muscatine, Illinois. Then after fleeing to Mexico to hide out for a few years, he came to Eureka Springs to start his reign of terror all over again. New Place. New faces. Same modus operandi.

If you want to know about Baker, look no further than the giant trove of articles and books on his life. In 2012, the Crescent went so far to have a one-man show about him. The following is an excerpt from the event's press release:

> *Starting on Friday, November 18, the character of Norman Baker will be brought to life in an hour-long theatrical presentation entitled* Midnight Theatre in the Morgue of the Mastermind: Norman Baker Speaks. *This intimate portrayal of this flamboyant, dynamic character will take place in The Crescent's "Faculty Lounge" of this proud member of Historic Hotels of America.*
>
> *The creator, writer, producer and star of this one-man multi-media show is award-winning actor Keith Scales, formerly of Portland (OR). Scales' exhaustive research on Baker will allow him to present Baker's story from Baker's perspective as Baker himself.*
>
> *The hour-long production finishes in the hotel's macabre morgue, a leftover from the Baker Hospital days, and will leave it up to members of the audience to decide if this native of Muscatine, Iowa, was a genius or a charlatan.*

As I scoured the internet, books and archives for any kind of evidence of the lives of the patients who lived through the pain, strife and the abuse of Baker and his fake medical hospital, I found that it's a desolate wasteland.

Part of this could be due to the fact that a lot of the records for the wellness center were burned or buried outside the hotel during one its renovations. At least that's the story that is being repeated. When the cachet of jars was found during the renovations of the back end of the hotel, there were other things discovered, including paraphernalia from the hospital. So, it could very well be that there just isn't any kind of paper trail for the patients who lived there.

The other concerning aspect of how the hospital conducted business is how people died there. Patients were promised that they would be cured

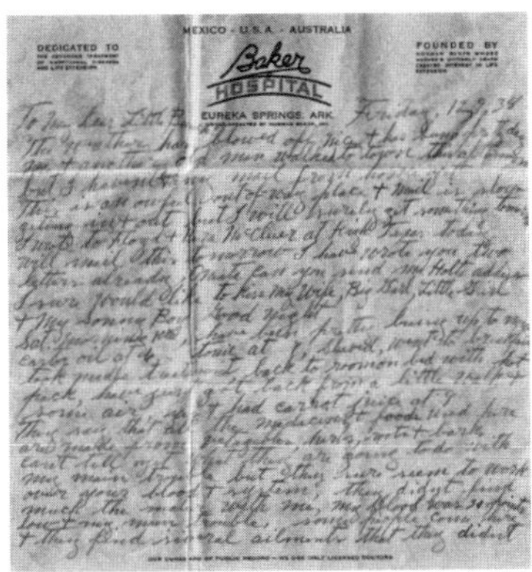

MEXICO · U.S.A. · AUSTRALIA

Baker HOSPITAL

EUREKA SPRINGS, ARK.

Letter by Luther J. Baggett. *Courtesy of the Crescent Hotel.*

within three to six weeks with the consistent injections of the magical "formula #5" solution. The protocol was gruesome. Nurses would inject the actual tumorous areas with the liquid without any kind of painkiller or anesthesia. It is said you could hear the screams of the patients being injected throughout the hallways.

Others were in so much pain and agony that they were put on the third floor and barricaded away from the other patients so they couldn't be heard. It was important to keep up the façade that people were being cured and leaving, that the hospital was a place of rest, relaxation and healing.

Unfortunately, that wasn't the case. When a patient began deteriorating, Baker would have them sent home to keep the death rate down so he could proclaim that nearly no one died in the wellness center. I mean, it was true. There are only forty-four deaths recorded at the hospital during the three years it was open. Those bodies ended up in the morgue and were stored in the giant freezer. Baker was said to never do any kind of surgery. At least that's the official story.

If someone was close to death and couldn't go home, Baker had them write letters to their loved ones so he could mail them posthumously and keep collecting the fees for treatment. A lot of times, families didn't know their relatives had died until months afterward, when they wanted to visit or took to doing their own research.

All this is to say that record-keeping was not the top priority of Baker and his staff. He did not care much for his patients or their well-being. The hotel changed hands many times, and I'm sure that at the time, no one realized how important the remnants of Baker's time were, especially to those who died or were sent home and never thought of again.

Fortunately, there is one piece of history that still exists. A letter from a cancer patient was given to the Crescent Hotel. His descendants found the letter and thought it was important that his voice was heard.

His name was Luther J. Baggett. He entered the cancer center sometime in the later months of 1938. The letter's date is December 9, 1938; he died just a couple of months later. His death date on Ancestry.com is listed as February 24, 1939. Bagget's letter was sent to his family in Lakeside, Arizona.

The following is the full transcription:

Friday, 12/9/1938
My Dear Little Bunch,

The weather has blowed off nice & has been a pretty day. Me & another old man walked to town this afternoon but I haven't had any mail from home yet. This is an awful out of way place & mail is slow getting in & out but I will surely get something tomorrow. I wrote to Floyd and Vera McCluer at High Texas today. Will mail this tomorrow. I have wrote you two letters already. Onaeta can you send me Holts address. I sure would like to kiss my wife, Big Girl, Little Girl, & My Sonny Boy. Good night.

Saturday morning, 10th. Have been pretty busy up to now. Castor oil at 6, tonic at 7, shaved, went to breakfast, took needle treatment back to room on bed with hot pack, have just got back from a little walk & some air, yes & had carrot juice at 9. They say that all the medicines & food used here are made from vegetables, herbs, roots & bark. Can't tell yet what they are going to do with my main trouble but they sure seem to work over your blood & system. They didn't find much the mater [sic] *with me, my blood was 30 points low, and my main trouble. Some people come here & they find several ailments that they didn't know they had. That makes it more expensive. One man came just ahead of me with several ailments & they charged him $500.00 flat rate for 5 weeks treatment without room, some are saving some money rooming out but they wanted me here in the hospital, it seems that most of them has to stay as much as five weeks & some longer since the mails seem so slow you had better let me know soon how you think we are going to get along financially. Guess I will try to stay the three weeks, if I don't stay any longer (I have $47.00 now). It will take $3.00 more for next week, $50.00 for the next & about $30.00 for a ticket & a little for laundry. About $90.00 more for three weeks, this sure has been a long week for me & since I haven't had a letter & wondering if some of you are bad sick, am going to try to write to Mamie today & I am not sure of her address.*

Well, the last mail has come for this week & I didn't get a letter don't know what to think & it seems there is nothing I can do about it. Will quit & get this in the mail.

Love to all,
LJB (Luther J. Baggett)

This letter shows a snapshot of what it was like staying at the cancer center. There was a lot of focus on treatment and cost. The wellness techniques he described are some that are used today, but they are used as parts of health maintenance. Not as the entire cure.

You can feel this man's frustration and desperation. You can tell he wants to get better and that he is willing to do anything to make that happen. I think the most heart-wrenching part is that he keeps talking about the mail. He's feeling alone out in the middle of the Ozark woods. He's waiting for the mail so that he has connection to his family. This man was lonely and dying. He was craving connection.

I'm sure his is just one story of many trapped in the chaos of time passing. His memory has been thrown into a pile of rubble and burned like a piece of trash. The only thing left of him is a handwritten letter on the lavender stationary of a man who didn't care about anything but money. At the end, it seems Baggett's life was little more than a transaction.

I want to leave you with this piece that my friend and colleague Stephanie wrote about her time at the Crescent Hotel. It beautifully encapsulates what we seem to forget about haunted hotels and the memories that lurk within. Please make sure to check out her work at www.stephaniecarrell.com.

Real Stories Lost in Time: The Crescent Experience, by Stephanie Carrell

I first discovered the Crescent Hotel in 2014 while planning a weekend getaway. I wasn't looking for anything haunted—just a place with history and charm. I love old hotels, and when I came across the Crescent on a booking site, I instantly knew it was the one I wanted to visit when I finally made it to Eureka Springs.

Three years later, I found out it was haunted when I saw a brochure for the ghost tour. Shortly after, Heather, who I'd met the year I discovered the Crescent, had posted a short video tour of the hotel for her followers, sharing some of the history and her impressions. That sparked more curiosity.

Still, I didn't make it there until 2021. That first visit was with Heather and a group of paranormal investigators. We stayed in room 419, Theodora's room. In 2022, my husband and I met up with Heather at the Crescent. Both visits were powerful in their own ways, but that first trip left me energetically wiped. I walked out of that hotel tired in a way that went far beyond just being short on sleep.

Room 419 would become a central point of our experience—the turquoise walls, the delicate gold stars painted on the walls. As the activity began to coalesce, Heather pulled out her planchette for automatic writing. The message was clear: go downstairs. When we ran out of paper, we turned to the Ouija board. I didn't use the board. I was the one keeping notes on what came through. Many of the messages were unclear, and we determined that the spirit we were talking to was not familiar with how to properly navigate to the letters on the board (pointing with the tip of the planchette versus placing the letter in the interior of the open circle). One of the most explicit messages was the word *red* and the name Max, which came right after we asked about the dumbwaiter in the closet. Again, we were told to go downstairs. The energy felt intelligent. Purposeful. There was a presence there—not intrusive but observant. Something aware of us.

When we returned the following year, the room was occupied. We spent time nearby, and I found myself pulled toward its windows over and over again. Later, we sat outside the door with a ghost box. Words like *rose* and *birthday* came through, though nothing definitive emerged. Still, there was a sense that something remembered us. Something wanted us to return.

I never felt touched or pushed in Room 419, but the space itself felt alert. If I had to describe the energy in one word: *watchful*. The most intense experience I've ever had at the Crescent didn't happen in 419. It occurred in one of the suites on the third floor.

We began our investigation in the hallway. As soon as we started walking down the stairs, I was hit with dizziness. The sensation of the floor shifting beneath my feet. I could feel the weight of the sadness pressing in—grief and despair from the people who had been left to suffer.

Heather was using dowsing rods to guide the group. They pointed us toward a specific suit. Something wanted us to go inside. I stayed outside in the hallway at first, performing an EVP session while others went in. After a while, I was invited into the room. I walked over to the area where the group had been focused. I was directed toward the window to get a sense of the energy in the space.

I placed my hands on the frame. I inhaled deeply, and it felt as if something entered me. I wasn't afraid, but I wasn't myself either. I began sobbing these deep, uncontrollable sobs that didn't belong to me. I could feel the emotions—despair, hopelessness—but I wasn't feeling them as me. I was the witness. The conduit.

Heather asked questions while I stood there, staring out toward the trees and the church steeple in the distance. I didn't focus on anything—I just looked. I didn't want to be there anymore. I wanted to go home.

My body began to feel as if it was swaying front and back, even though I was standing solidly on the floor, my hands still on the windowsill. Then I felt as if I were falling forward, out the window.

The channeling ended as suddenly as it began. I was back. Still dizzy, still shaken, but me again. We resumed the dowsing session, and the story emerged. The woman hadn't jumped. She hadn't been pushed. She'd been sedated—drugged—and in an incoherent, vulnerable state, she fell.

She wasn't angry. She was lost. Trapped in the same hopelessness that had shaped her life. Her story—her truth—had been buried beneath layers of ghost lore and tourist tales, overshadowed by the myths. She's still there, not to haunt. She's there because her story was never finished.

That same night, following the messages from room 419 and the event in the suite, we made our way to the basement to investigate the hallway leading to the morgue. It was dark, and the farther we walked, the denser and heavier the space felt.

Halfway down the hallway, we stopped and set up our Estes session. A childlike presence came through first. We sensed it might be tied to the remains stored in one of the jars in the morgue. During the session, another presence made itself known. Stronger. Heavier. Darker. It tried to dominate the space. It wasn't evil, just confrontational. When it saw it couldn't intimidate us, it left.

We also experienced the smell of ether wafting through the air.

The hallway doesn't feel like a place of trauma, but it is alive with movement. I think of it more as a transition zone. A cauldron, or womb space. A place where spirits pass through, not necessarily where they stay. I believe that's due to the energy of the land itself—the minerals, the flowing water, the very bones of the mountain. It's a magnet for spiritual activity.

I would absolutely go back there alone. Not for the thrill—just to sit and listen.

The most heartbreaking part of the Crescent is the silence around the real people who suffered there. The hotel capitalizes on their suffering, but it does little to honor them. The patients from the Baker era have been reduced to spooky anecdotes, their real stories lost to time.

Yet their energy is still there. Especially on the second and third floors—the areas added during the hospital years. So many people were brought there under false hope and left to suffer and die. The trauma is still embedded in the walls.

Some spirits are residual, looping through the pain of their final moments. But others are still waiting, hoping someone will see them. Someone will listen.

As for Norman Baker? I don't believe he's lingering. Nothing is tethering him to that place. He never cared—not about patients, not about the hospital. He was a showman, and when the light went out, he moved on, emotionless, remorseless. There's no reason for him to stay.

Is the Crescent haunted? Without a doubt.

I believe everyone who walks into that place feels something, whether they realize it or not. There's a chaotic energy that unsettles you. Most people don't know what to do with it, so they numb it—with food, with alcohol, with anything that keeps them from feeling too much. And in doing so, they open themselves up to even more.

For me, the most profound moments came not in fear but in empathy. I don't seek to provoke or command spirits. I want to witness, to hold space, to remember.

If you visit the Crescent, go there with respect and go where you're pulled. If you listen more than you speak, you might just catch a glimpse of something real from places you didn't expect.

TRAIL OF TEARS PARK

1100 Martin Luther King Jr. Boulevard
Fayetteville, Arkansas 72701

Tucked into a surprisingly quiet corner of Fayetteville, at the intersection of Martin Luther King Jr. Boulevard and Garland Avenue, sits Trail of Tears Park. It's a small park, four and a half landscaped acres on the edge of the University of Arkansas's campus, but the weight of what happened here is massive.

This exact location was once an encampment site. On January 13, 1839, around 1,200 Cherokee people stopped here as part of the Benge detachment. It was bitterly cold. Many were sick. Some were dying. They camped near the water source that still runs across the street, parallel to the road and recreation trail. Today there's a stone sculpture and a plaque planted among native trees and grasses, commemorating their presence.

It's peaceful. That's the strangest thing. You stand there, the traffic buzzes behind you, students walk by with backpacks, and it feels like the world has moved on. And it has. But the ground remembers.

The park is open to the public Monday through Friday, from 8:00 a.m. to 5:00 p.m. It's free. There's no big fanfare. You could drive by it one hundred times and never stop. But you should stop.

Stand there. Read the plaque. Look at the trees. Remember what happened on this land. Not in theory—in this exact spot.

TRAIL OF TEARS: THE HISTORY THAT HIDES IN PLAIN SIGHT

If you live in Northwest Arkansas, you've probably heard the phrase "Trail of Tears." Maybe you learned about it in high school. Maybe you passed one of the brown historical markers while on a scenic drive and barely glanced at it. Maybe you've never given it much thought beyond the vague idea that "bad things happened to Natives once."

The Trail of Tears wasn't just a dark chapter in American history. It was a deliberate, calculated act of ethnic cleansing. A mass forced migration. A slow-moving genocide. And it happened right here, across this very land we now jog on, bike through and develop into luxury condos.

Fayetteville was once a stopover for thousands of Cherokee people forcibly removed from their ancestral homes. This isn't a distant event. This is local history. And it still echoes underfoot.

In 1830, President Andrew Jackson signed the Indian Removal Act into law, which effectively gave the federal government permission to uproot Indigenous nations from their land east of the Mississippi. The goal was to relocate them to Indian Territory, which would become present-day Oklahoma. This was done in the name of progress. But the path west was brutal.

Starting in the late 1830s, tens of thousands of Cherokee, Creek, Choctaw, Chickasaw and Seminole people were rounded up, often at gunpoint, and sent on foot, by wagon or by boat across hundreds of miles. The Cherokee called it *Nunna daul Tsuny*, or The Trail Where They Cried.

Over four thousand Cherokee people died on that journey from exhaustion, exposure, starvation and disease. Some froze to death. Some gave birth on the side of the road. Children died in their mothers' arms. Entire families were wiped out before reaching Indian Territory.

Here in Northwest Arkansas, they passed through Cane Hill, Prairie Grove, Springdale, Fayetteville and beyond. Wagons creaked along what's now U.S. Route 62. Camps were set up outside town boundaries, and makeshift burial grounds were left behind. Some of those routes are now roads you drive on every day.

The truth is that much of modern Northwest Arkansas was made possible because of this mass removal. Once the Native people were gone, the land was divvied up, surveyed and sold. Settlers built homes. Churches. Feed stores. And history moved on—at least for those who didn't have to carry its weight.

A ROUTE WORTH RIDING

If you want to go deeper, there's a bike route designed to take you to key sites along the Trail of Tears. You can bring your own bike or rent one through the VeoRide Bikeshare Program, which offers regular and pedal-assist bikes at stations around town.

Here's the suggested itinerary:

Stop 1: Trail of Tears Park
1100 Martin Luther King Jr. Boulevard
Fayetteville, Arkansas 72701

Start here. Ground yourself. Read the exhibit materials. Notice the creek nearby. Imagine hundreds of people gathered around fires, cold, hungry and uncertain about where they were going.

Stop 2: Tsa La Gi Trail

Just across the street from the park is Tsa La Gi trail. *Tsa-La-Gi* is the Cherokee word for "Cherokee." This trail segment roughly follows the original removal route. It's a well-maintained path now a part of the Razorback Greenway, but it overlays a route built on suffering. You'll ride alongside the very geography the Cherokee once walked.

Stop 3: Sarah Ridge House
230 West Center Street
Fayetteville, Arkansas 72701

Sarah Ridge was the widow of Major Ridge, a Cherokee leader who was assassinated in Indian Territory for signing the Treaty of New Echota, which ceded Cherokee land to the U.S. government. After his death, Sarah fled Oklahoma and settled in Fayetteville. Her log home still exists, encased within the modern structure on this property. You can't go inside, but there's an exhibit outside worth seeing.

Stop 4: Site of Fayetteville Female Seminary
301 West Mountain Street
Fayetteville, Arkansas 72701

Founded in 1839 by Sophia Sawyer, a missionary who worked with the Cherokee, this school was one of the few institutions that educated Native girls during and after removal. It's a reminder that some people did care and tried to help. But even those efforts were shaped by colonization and assimilation ideals.

Stop 5: Fayetteville Square Gardens
1 West Center Street
Fayetteville, Arkansas 72701

End your ride downtown. Maybe grab a tea, sit on a bench and let it all sink in. This was once a surveying hub. The lots here were laid out in 1835, just before removal began in earnest. Everything around you was built on land cleared by federal policy.

The Experience Fayetteville Visitor Center is here, too, and it can help you navigate back or plan more stops if you're feeling inspired.

Beyond Fayetteville: Building a Wider Route

If you want to explore even more Trail of Tears sites throughout Northwest Arkansas, you can. It's not all neatly labeled on a map, and a lot of it isn't obvious, but that's the point. The trail is there. Still.

Here are a few other locations tied to the route:

- Cane Hill: The trail passed directly through this tiny town. Check out Cane Hill Cemetery and see if you can spot any older graves connected to the 1830s.

- Prairie Grove Battlefield State Park: While this site is known for its Civil War history, this site also sits near parts of the trail route. The landscape is layered in trauma.

- Van Buren: Several detachments passed through here along the Arkansas River. Some boat routes also used the river as a transport corridor.

- Pea Ridge National Military Park: This park is unrelated to the trail itself, but it provides a good sense of the terrain and how grueling traveling through the Ozarks would have been.

WHY THIS GETS LEFT OUT

So, why isn't any of this common knowledge? Why isn't it front and center in Fayetteville's glossy brochures or heritage signs? There's no single answer, but I can guess.

Part of it is white guilt. It's hard to hold parades and promote "pioneer heritage" when you have to acknowledge the land was cleared by force. It makes the narrative messy. Uncomfortable. And this region, like many, has gotten very good at polishing its image while leaving inconvenient truths in the shadows.

Another part of it is that these stories weren't passed down. They were deliberately erased. Native voices were pushed out geographically and historically. Public memory doesn't like to linger on pain it caused.

But ignoring it doesn't make it go away. The land remembers. And it will keep whispering until someone stops to listen.

Here's my ask, whether you're local, visiting, researching or just curious: don't let this be another marker you pass without stopping. Go to Trail of Tears Park. Walk the Tsa La Gi Trail. Look at the water running beside it, and imagine people dipping cloths into it to cool fevers. Picture the wagons. Hear the silence that followed them.

Tell someone about it. Because memory needs action. And silence protects only the wrong things.

We owe it to the people who walked this trail to see what's beneath our feet. It's not about guilt. It's about recognition. Acknowledgment. Deciding that some truths don't get to stay buried just because they're inconvenient.

The trail is still here. Let's not forget that.

CONCLUSION

Here's the thing about ghost towns: they never really leave.

Sure, the buildings collapse. The roads fade. The signs rust, the names disappear from maps, and nature takes it all back, like it always does. But the energy of these places—the people who lived, died, dreamed and despaired there—doesn't just vanish. It settles. It sleeps. It waits.

While writing this book, walking through broken foundations and overgrown trails, reading microfiche until my eyes blurred, I kept thinking one thing: none of this is truly gone. It just stopped being seen.

That's the tricky part about forgotten places. They're not always hidden. Sometimes, they're right there on the side of the road. Sometimes, you pass them every day and don't notice. Or maybe you do notice—a strange chimney in a field, an out-of-place staircase in the woods, a lone graveyard fenced in like it's protecting something—and you feel a flicker of something, but you keep driving. Because you don't know what it is. Because there's no sign. Because nobody told you the story.

That's why I wrote this. Not just to tell you what happened. But to remind you that something did.

One of the weird things about writing a book like this is that people expect every place to have some grand reason it mattered. Like it needs a major historical event, a famous death or a presidential speech to be worth remembering.

But that's not what this book is about. This book is about places that mattered because people lived there. That's enough. It's about the towns that quietly went broke. The communities swallowed by lakes. The buildings too expensive to save. The hospitals full of stories no one wanted to tell anymore. It's about lives lived between the lines of "official history," the small things, the personal things, the haunted things. The messy, unremarkable, human parts.

I'm not here to glorify ruin. This isn't about romanticizing decay. It's about recognizing what gets erased when we move too fast. What gets lost when a story doesn't fit the narrative we want to tell about ourselves or our region.

These forgotten places aren't relics. They're reminders. The land remembers, even if we don't.

There's something about the Ozarks, something older than roads and rooftops. You feel it when the fog rolls in low and thick over a field you can't name. When a crow lands on a fence post and stares a little too long. When the wind cuts through a holler and sounds almost like a voice.

These hills have held everything—wars, settlements, epidemics, secret societies, backroom deals, bootlegging routes, sanctuaries, graveyards, broken dreams. And they hold all of it like a rumor that might still be true if you're brave enough to listen.

Northwest Arkansas, for all its growth and gentrification, still has shadows. You just have to look past the coffee shops and new developments. Look down. Look sideways. Look at the places that don't make it onto postcards anymore.

When a town dies, it's never just the economy or the population that disappears. It's the culture. The stories. The way people spoke. The songs they sang. The dishes they cooked. The weird little traditions that made no sense to anyone outside the county line.

And when we stop telling those stories, when we let the buildings rot and don't bother to ask what happened, we lose something more than land. We lose identity. We lose continuity. We lose the lessons that history whispers, not the ones it yells.

Every town in this book was built by someone who believed in something. Even if it was just a better life. A little more space. Cleaner air. A miracle cure. A second chance. And maybe they didn't get what they came for. Maybe it all went sideways. But they were here. They tried.

That deserves to be remembered.

I've spent enough time in these places to know that when the air shifts, when a place is holding onto something, you don't have to believe in ghosts to feel it. But I do. And I'll say this: some places don't want to be forgotten.

I've been followed. I've been watched. I've walked into buildings where the silence is too quiet. I've heard doors slam where there were no doors. I felt the temperature drop like someone exhaled right behind me. Even the skeptic in me doesn't ignore that.

And that's part of the reason I feel so strongly about preserving what we can. These places are still alive in some way. They're holding energy. Holding memory. And sometimes, they hold grief.

If you're reading this and thinking, "Wow, now I want to go see some of these places." Good. That's the point.

Go take the drive. Go walk the gravel roads. Pull over when you see a boarded-up building and wonder what it used to be. Look for the cemeteries tucked behind overgrown brush. Ask questions. Talk to the locals. Visit the tiny museums. Support the preservation efforts, even if that means just sharing a photo or telling a friend about something weird you saw out near Calico Rock.

Because the more we talk about these places, the less forgotten they become. And don't wait for someone else to document it. You don't need to be a historian or an expert to care. If something pulls you in, follow it. That's how all of this started for me. A feeling. A nudge. A name on a map I didn't recognize.

This book isn't comprehensive. It's not meant to be. There are hundreds of places I didn't get to, dozens more things I didn't know about until after I finished writing. And plenty of stories are still buried out there, waiting for someone else to pick up the thread.

So, maybe that's where you come in. Because this land is full of stories. And it's not done telling them. Not even close. We're just lucky enough to be listening.

So, here's to the ghost towns, the lost places, the ones that slipped between the cracks. Here's to the silence that hums louder the longer you stand still. Here's to the stories that won't let go.

And here's to the ones still waiting to be found.

BIBLIOGRAPHY

Websites

Beck, Ginger. "Peppersauce, AR." Abandoned AR. December 3, 2018. https://abandonedar.com/peppersauce-ar.

Blevins, Bill Dwayne. "Rush (Marion County)." *Encyclopedia of Arkansas*. July 22, 2023. https://encyclopediaofarkansas.net/entries/rush-ghost-town-marion-county-1270.

Boerner, Talya Tate. "Calico Rock Ghost Town." Only in Arkansas. October 1, 2015. https://onlyinark.com/places-and-travel/thriller-thursday-calico-rock-ghost-town.

Bopp, Ron. "Norman Baker (A Life History)." Carousel Organ, no. 28, July 2006. https://coaa.us/index_archive/Issues_21_to_30/Norman%20Baker%20(A%20Life%20History)_%20Ron%20Bopp_%20_28%20&%2029.pdf.

Bowden, Bill. "Glass Bottles Found Behind 'Haunted' Arkansas Hotel Date to 1938 Cancer Elixir." *Arkansas Democrat Gazette*, April 12, 2019. https://www.arkansasonline.com/news/2019/apr/12/glass-bottles-date-to-38-cancer-elixir-.

"Brunckow Cabin." Tombstone Travel Tips. https://www.tombstonetraveltips.com/brunckow-cabin.html.

Carter, Mark. "Second Act Forthcoming: Dogpatch USA Awaits Its Remake." AMP. December 13, 2023. https://armoneyandpolitics.com/dogpatch-usa-awaits-its-remake.

Comer, Gt. "Peppersauce Ghost Town." Atlas Obscura. May 10, 2016. https://www.atlasobscura.com/places/peppersauce-ghost-town.

"Crescent Hotel: Haunted by History and Haints." Ozarks Alive. September 29, 2023. https://www.ozarksalive.com/stories/crescenthoteleurekasprings.

Davis, Kayla. "A Look Inside War Eagle Cavern's Expansion, Historic Discovery." KNWA News. March 3, 2023. https://www.nwahomepage.com/news/war-eagle-cavern-expansion-leads-to-historic-discovery.

"Dogpatch USA." Wikipedia. https://en.wikipedia.org/wiki/Dogpatch_USA.

Dougan, Michael B. "Norman Baker (1882–1958)." *Encyclopedia of Arkansas.* December 21, 2023. https://encyclopediaofarkansas.net/entries/norman-baker-4885.

"Explore the Ghost Town or Rush." Somewhere in Arkansas. January 27, 2024. https://somewhereinarkansas.com/ghost-town-of-rush-arkansas.

Hales, James F. "War Eagle Sites Mill History from 1840s." *Arkansas Democrat Gazette*, December 8, 2016. https://www.arkansasonline.com/news/2016/dec/08/war-eagle-sites-mill-history-from-1840s.

"History of Arkansas." *Encyclopedia of Britannica.* 2023. https://www.britannica.com/place/Arkansas-state/History.

Johnson, Melanie. "This Fascinating Arkansas Town Has Been Abandoned and Reclaimed by Nature for Decades Now." Only in Arkansas. February 15, 2003. https://www.onlyinyourstate.com/experiences/arkansas/abandoned-and-reclaimed-by-ar.

Killerlane, John. "Con Man: The Fraud Who Claimed to Have a Cure for Cancer." History Collection. October 30, 2017. https://historycollection.com/norman-baker-man-claimed-cure-cancer.

Meador, Granger. "Before Jurassic Park Came Farwells." Meador.org. February 7, 2024. https://meador.org/2024/02/07/before-jurassic-park-came-farwells.

Mitchell, Kimberly. "War Eagle Mill: An Arkansas Icon." Only in Arkansas. October 17, 2024. https://onlyinark.com/places-and-travel/war-eagle-mill.

"Monte Ne." Wikipedia. https://en.wikipedia.org/wiki/Monte_Ne.

"Mystery Solved!" Crescent Hotel & Spa. 2024. https://crescent-hotel.com/blog/press-releases/mystery-solved.

"Norman Baker Comes Back to Life." Crescent Hotel & Spa. September 29, 2012. https://crescent-hotel.com/blog/norman-baker-comes-back-to-life/.

Schwarz, Michael. "Dinosaur World." Abandoned AR. February 9, 2013. https://abandonedar.com/dinosaur-world.

———. "Dogpatch USA." Abandoned AR. January 4, 2014. https://abandonedar.com/dogpatch-usa.

Scoobysleuth. "Rush Ghost Town." Atlas Obscura. October 26, 2014. https://www.atlasobscura.com/places/rush-ghost-town.

Shirleytwofeathers. "Zinc Magick." Magickal Ingredients. September 27, 2016. https://shirleytwofeathers.com/The_Blog/magickal-ingredients/zinc.

"Ultimate Guide to War Eagle Cavern, Arkansas (Tours, Pricing, History, Map)." World of Caves. https://worlofcaves.com/ultimate-guide-to-war-eagle-cavern-arkansas-tours-pricing-history-map.

"Uncovering the Past: The Baker Hospital Through the Eyes of a Patient." Crescent Hotel & Spa. February 15, 2022. https://crescent-hotel.com/blog/uncovering-the-past.

"The Underwater Ruins in Monte Ne are a Strange Sight in Arkansas." Only in Your State. September 18, 2019. https://www.onlyinyourstate.com/arkansas/monte-ne-underwater-ruins.

VanDyke, J.B. "Most People Have No Idea This Unique Abandoned Park in Arkansas Exists." Only in Arkansas. September 22, 2023. https://www.onlyinyourstate.com/experiences/arkansas/unique-abandoned-dino-park-ar.

"War Eagle, Arkansas." Wikipedia. https://en.wikipedia.org/wiki/War_Eagle,_Arkansas.

"War Eagle Mill." Wikipedia. https://en.wikipedia.org/wiki/War_Eagle_Mill.

"William Hope Harvey." Wikipedia. https://en.wikipedia.org/wiki/William_Hope_Harvey.

Books

Juhnke, Eric S. *Quacks and Crusaders: The Fabulous Careers of John Brinkley, Norman Baker, and Harry Hoxsey*. University Press of Kansas, 2002.

Lord, Allyn. *Historic Monte Ne*. Rogers Historical Museum, 2006.

Schaefer, Susan. *The Crescent Hotel with Ghost Stories*. Susan Schaefer, 2015.

Schwarz, Michael. *Abandoned Arkansas: An Echo from the Past*. America Through Time, 2019.

Videos

Flaxman, Larry. "Bottles from 1886 Crescent Hotel EXPOSED!" YouTube. September 30, 2022. https://www.youtube.com/watch?v=XhY9E-kaYkg.

ABOUT THE AUTHOR

Heather Woodward is a psychic, paranormal investigator and writer who has spent over two decades chasing ghosts, uncovering lost histories and asking questions most people are too polite—or too scared—to ask. Based in Northwest Arkansas, she specializes in exploring the forgotten corners of the Ozarks, where abandoned towns, haunted ruins and buried secrets still hum beneath the surface.

With a background in historical research, spiritual work and fringe phenomena, Heather blends fact, folklore and intuition to tell the stories that don't make it into textbooks. She's also the host of the *NVus Alien Podcast*, where she digs into conspiracies, high strangeness and the weird undercurrents of American history.

When she's not writing, podcasting or poking around a long-abandoned building, you'll find her sipping tea, creating tarot decks or communing with spirits, who tend to show up uninvited.

Ghost Towns and Forgotten Places of Northwest Arkansas is her latest deep dive into the quiet places time tried to erase and a love letter to the landscapes that still hold secrets—if you're willing to look.